Praise for *Teaching and Supporting Migrant Children in Our Schools: A Culturally Proficient Approach*

"Although often overlooked in schools and curricula, the children of farmworker families nonetheless bring rich cultural and linguistic strengths to their education. By describing how a culturally proficient framework can bridge the gap between migrant children and those entrusted with teaching them, Quezada, Rodríguez-Valls, and Lindsey make a compelling case that these children deserve an education that is culturally responsive, deeply engaging, and respectful of their particular sociocultural realities."

—**Sonia Nieto**, PhD, professor emerita, language, literacy, and culture, College of Education, University of Massachusetts, Amherst

"*Teaching and Supporting Migrant Children in Our Schools* offers educators, policy makers, and community-based organizations an engaging learning opportunity aimed at maximizing effective educational and social services to migrant student and their families in our schools and communities. It provides a compelling case for the reader to assume a leadership role as a change agent to affirmatively address the low academic achievement of migrant students in the educational system specifically and the plight of migrant families generally. It offers a comprehensive and culturally sensitive approach to the academic preparation of migrant students and empowerment of migrant parents in the educational process. My deepest gratitude to the authors for further documenting the educational needs of migrant students and encouraging the leadership actions required to change the educational and social circumstance of migrant students and families."

—**Rafael S. Hernandez**, director, Early Academic Outreach Program, University of California, San Diego

"I have had the pleasure of working in the Migrant Education Program for 46 years and can honestly say, this book is one of the best efforts in endeavoring to communicate how best to work with migrant students in the classroom. The research and suggested activities are realistic, doable, stimulating, and challenging."

—**Dr. Joe I. Mendoza**, director, Migrant Education Region 17; director, Special Populations Educational Support Department, Ventura County Office of Education

"We educators continue to strive to find ways to better serve the most at-risk students, who most of our migrant students tend to be. Part of that is due to their unique needs connected to their mobile lifestyle. Quezada, Rodríguez-Valls, and Lindsey in this book provide an accurate and comprehensive view of the migrant students and their families. These educators show us the great respect and hope for a better future that they have for this population. That future can only be accomplished by educators who know well their students and themselves. This book provides the academic tools and rubrics that can be used by any educator who believes in education as the avenue toward a better future. This is a must-read for anyone who is working with migrant students and families, as well anyone who wants to explore a constructive academic approach to better serve the neediest children in our schools."

—**Dr. Sandra Kofford**, director, Migrant Education Region 6, Imperial County Office of Education

"Quezada, Rodríguez-Valls, and Lindsey not only disclose the often-invisible population of migrant children in our schools but also stress the necessity that school system stakeholders must provide equitable educational opportunities for them in an inclusive environment. The authors are able to share how we, as educators, must first look within ourselves and offer in-text opportunities to deeply reflect on the 'inside-out approach' with journaling opportunities to analyze personal assumptions of migrant students. During this incredible shift in our nation's demographics and accountability, this text provides direction through an intersection where we can engage migrant students and their families."

—**Lori Piowlski**, PhD, assistant professor, Department of Elementary and
Early Childhood Education, Minnesota State University, Mankato

"Quezada, Rodríguez-Valls, and Lindsey have created an important resource for educators looking to understand and help our migrant students. As a former migrant student, I can appreciate the honesty and focus of this book, which will help all of our migrant students have greater success in their educational journey. This well-researched book provides coverage of a number of important issues and research not commonly considered in other textbooks."

—**Simon Silva**, artist, author, speaker

"*Teaching and Supporting Migrant Children in Our Schools: A Culturally Proficient Approach* will quickly become a pivotal work for both teacher candidates and experienced educators, inspiring readers to think deeply about current policies and practices in their schools of today. The chapters engage and move the teacher into immediate reflection to consider the trajectory of personal teaching practices: *What does it mean to be a culturally proficient teacher? What truly matters in my school? What values and behaviors do we communicate through our school's policies and practices? How can I move beyond my own cultural lens to embrace all cultures different than my own?* The authors use case stories as narratives to touch a deep place within to guide, encourage and challenge schools to embrace all students and families with purpose and impact. Even more, the Culturally Proficiency Rubric provides a framework to illuminate and guide the development of a school community that embraces inclusive and effective practices for all learners. Such a formative work will inspire educators into an engaged conversation and an openness to inclusive teaching practices—a critical conversation for all school communities in the 21st century!"

—**Janine F. Allen**, associate provost of global engagement, Corban University

"When I arrived in California fresh out of college with my 'Hispanic Studies' degree in hand, I wish I'd had this book in the other. It would have given much-needed introspection and intentionality to work I did with migrant youth and families both in and out of schools. Now that I'm in Iowa, I teach a course to prepare future educators here for their own work with the newcomer US Mexican community. This book can replace many of the resources that for years I've had to pull together to meet that course's needs. Its case-based orientation, cultural proficiency framework aligned to key school functions and leadership roles, and educators' rubrics for inclusion and support all serve to fill the gap between theory and practice that future educators expect. *Teaching and Supporting Migrant Children in Our Schools* is a critically important resource for ongoing learning towards transformative teaching, one that I will make sure my students don't leave their preparation program without."

—**Katherine Richardson Bruna**, PhD, director, Iowa State University

Teaching and Supporting Migrant Children in Our Schools

A Culturally Proficient Approach

Reyes L. Quezada,
Fernando Rodríguez-Valls,
and Randall B. Lindsey

ROWMAN & LITTLEFIELD
Lanham • Boulder • New York • London

Published by Rowman & Littlefield
A wholly owned subsidiary of The Rowman & Littlefield Publishing Group, Inc.
4501 Forbes Boulevard, Suite 200, Lanham, Maryland 20706
www.rowman.com

Unit A, Whitacre Mews, 26-34 Stannary Street, London SE11 4AB

British Library Cataloguing in Publication Information Available

Library of Congress Cataloging-in-Publication Data Available

ISBN: 978-1-4758-2111-6 (cloth : alk. paper)
ISBN: 978-1-4758-2112-3 (pbk. : alk. paper)
ISBN: 978-1-4758-2113-0 (electronic)

♾™ The paper used in this publication meets the minimum requirements of American
National Standard for Information Sciences—Permanence of Paper for Printed Library
Materials, ANSI/NISO Z39.48-1992.

Printed in the United States of America

This book is dedicated:

To my family—my wife, Cynthia, my son, Raymundo Reyes, and my daughter, Kristina Belen, who continue to surprise me with their accomplishments!

&

To my father, Jose Timoteo Quezada, who worked tirelessly in agriculture as a farmworker throughout the United States. To my sisters, Maria, Dolores, Amparo, and my three brothers, Ruben, Salvador, and my twin Efrain—Gracias, as we all worked in the California agricultural fields as an honorable job to help support the family and learned much from it. A special thank you to my mother, Belen, and to my younger brother, Raymundo, whom I am sure would have done great things in this world!

—Reyes

To all the migrant students and families who continuously challenge me to design culturally and linguistically responsive programs.

—Fernando

To the educators at Kewanee High School, Illinois for their inclusive practices. My acknowledgment is to Delores B. Lindsey for her advice and feedback during all stages in the development of this project.

—Randy

Contents

Foreword

"Children of the road" is what migrant students are often called. The sons and daughters of migrant agricultural workers, these children are defined by their mobility, a mobility which means that they suffer disrupted and interrupted education, often leaving school before the end of the school year in the spring and returning to school after the year has begun in the late summer or fall. These children often attend multiple schools each year as their parents travel to find agricultural work in the fields and orchards of the United States. They experience a patchwork quilt of education, a quilt which sometimes has a quilt square missing here or there.

Migrant farmworkers have been called the poorest of the working poor. They often travel long distances to find extremely low-paying jobs, many times earning below the minimum wage. Their wages are so low that they and their families are often hungry. Their housing is generally dilapidated and poorly constructed, and they often live with other families in overcrowded conditions. Many workers live in what are called labor camps, a kind of barracks-style housing where showers and sanitary facilities can be outdoors and separate from sleeping quarters. They work in the very hot sun in unimaginably difficult conditions. Farmworkers are often exposed to toxic pesticides that lead to many health problems, including cancer.

Farmworkers are very hard working in spite of the terrible working and living conditions they endure on a daily basis. They are family oriented and want to make a better future for their children. They are often said to embody the American dream or ideal, yet the vast majority are marginalized and treated poorly, and their work and contribution to the economy and to the country not fully appreciated.

Migrant farmworkers often have low levels of educational attainment and consequently suffer from very low levels of literacy. Many farmworkers are not fluent in English and a fairly large percentage of them are immigrants, including some with no documentation. Due to these circumstances, many farmworkers are not able to help their children with homework or assist them with choosing courses or a path of academic studies, and they do not understand how a child might apply and be admitted to post-secondary education.

Migrant children are, therefore, often on their own in their academic studies. While they may appear to share the characteristics of many other children in public schools—very low income, being a member of a racial or ethnic minority, being an English learner, and lacking academic support at home—they suffer from an additional characteristic, which is absolutely key to the challenges they face in school: their mobility.

Dr. Robert Coles, the highly regarded Harvard psychiatrist, published a series of books, essentially studies, on a number of different groups of children. Called "Children of Crisis," one of those studies focused on migrant children. Dr. Coles found much in these children years ago that still holds true today. They suffer significant emotional distress from the lack of permanency in their lives, from the fact that they are uprooted, from their lack of acceptance among their peers as they travel from school to school, and, in recent years, from fears attendant to immigration enforcement that affect migrant families and others in their communities. These issues compound the challenges they already face in achieving academic success.

In 1965, as part of the War on Poverty, President Lyndon Baines Johnson signed into law the Elementary and Secondary Education Act (ESEA). This statute provided new federally funded support to supplement what local school districts were providing in areas with concentrations of low-income students. One year later, in 1966, recognizing that the programs that were established by the ESEA did not address the needs of mobile migrant students who were the children of migrant farmworkers, Congress added what is currently called the Title I, Part C, Migrant Education Program.

This program was established to provide states with additional resources to serve migrant students, mandating that these states engage in interstate coordination and cooperation to support and assist these children as they travel from school district to school district, from state to state. What has developed from this very effective program is the strengthening of that national quilt for migrant students, leading to credit accrual programs allowing states and local districts to piece together school work done in several districts and states so that migrant children might complete courses and graduate from high school, and supplemental instruction to bridge the gaps that migrant children suffer due to their missing school as a result of their mobility, among many other services.

While school districts are required to provide supplemental instruction to these students through what is today called Title I, Part A (the program first

established in 1965), the challenges specifically created by these students'
mobility is bridged by this additional supplemental program, the Migrant
Education Program. The Migrant Education Program is responsible for
reducing the extraordinary drop-out rate suffered by these children in the
assisting with a variety of academic support as the students travel, and providing dedicated migrant education staff who understand both the academic and
emotional challenges facing these children.

Migrant children are often neglected in schools as they are in society. This
very important book co-authored by Reyes Quezada, Fernando Rodríguez-
Valls, and Randy Lindsey focuses on how schools, administrators, teachers,
and other school personnel can meet the educational and emotional needs
of migrant students. The book provides a variety of paths to meeting the
challenges faced by migrant students in the classroom and the quest of these
students for equal access to a quality education, an education to which they
have a legal and moral right.

The lessons taught when ensuring the educational rights of migrant students are equally applicable to other children of color, as well as other low-
income students who might be marginalized in school or in society. It is to be
hoped that use of this book in schools and school districts around the country
will go a long way to even the playing field for migrant students, ensuring
them a full opportunity to learn, to succeed, and to fulfill their promise and
their dreams.

Roger C. Rosenthal, Esq.
Executive Director
Migrant Legal Action Program
Washington, DC

Acknowledgments

A special thanks to all of the expert panelists for taking the time to review and provide feedback on the *Educators' Rubric for Inclusion and Support of Migrant Education Students, Their Families, and Their Communities.* Your work is truly appreciated.

Dr. Viviana Alexandrowicz, Associate Professor, University of San Diego

Dr. Oscar Jimenez-Castellanos, Associate Professor, Arizona State University

Dr. Karen Cadiero-Kaplan, Professor, San Diego State University

Dr. Frank Davila, Binational Migrant Students, INET

Dr. Sandra Kofford, Migrant Education Program Director, Region 6

Dr. Joe Mendoza, Director of the Special Populations Educational Support Department Ventura County Office of Education

Elena Morales, Teacher, Heber Elementary School District

Dr. Lori Piowlski, Assistant Professor, Minnesota State University-Mankato

Dr. Gregorio Ponce, Interim Dean, San Diego State University IV Campus

Dr. Patricia Perez, Associate Professor, California State University, Fullerton

Shantall Porchia, Migrant Education Program Coordinator, Region 8

Dr. Maria Estela Zárate, Associate Professor, California State University, Fullerton

Part I

TOOLS TO SUPPORT YOUR EFFECTIVE USE OF THIS BOOK

This book is designed to support your professional learning. Throughout this book you are provided thinking prompts to capture your ideas and "ahas," to record questions, and, sometimes, just to doodle. So, you are invited to select a journal format that best meets your learning style and needs. It might be that you will select a traditional bound paper journal (single or double entry), a spiral notebook, a digital format on your computer or tablet, or some other format you have devised—what is important is that you select the journal approach that best meets your needs.

Each chapter in the book has three types of strategically placed prompts designed to provoke your thinking, so please use them. You will see prompts for individual educator use and prompts intended to promote dialogue with colleagues. Once you get to one of these prompts, you will be invited to turn to your journal and respond to the prompt. Here are the types of "Opportunity to Journal" prompts:

- *Getting Centered*—Each chapter begins with a "Getting Centered" prompt designed to whet your thinking about the content for that chapter. Use these prompts to get you started in "thinking about your thinking." Our intent with these prompts is to create an anticipatory mindset for the chapter.
- *Reflection*—Throughout the chapters, you are invited to, under the head "Reflections," summarize salient points and to record your reactions and assumptions. Engaging you with the content this way provides opportunity for you to integrate the chapter material with your ever-evolving pedagogy and praxis.
- *Case Stories*—Throughout the chapters, case stories are presented as composite conversations among pre-K–12 educators with whom the authors have associated. These case stories serve to illustrate the tools of cultural

1

proficiency and provide readers opportunity for reflection and dialogue about their own practice.
- *Going Deeper*—The chapters end with "Going Deeper," which provide an opportunity for you to reflect on the content of the chapter. The purpose of "Going Deeper" is to inform your practice with the use of the values, content, and skills gained from the chapter.
- *Dialogic Activity*—The chapters end with "Dialogic Activity," which provides prompts for engaging with colleagues. The purpose of "Dialogic Activity" is for colleagues to understand one another's perspectives on the use of the content, values, and skills in serving the academic and social needs of your diverse student population.

Our Rationale

Across the United States and Canada, staff or professional development programs are implemented where too often something done "to" participants has evolved into being about educators' professional learning.

Learning Forward, a national association devoted to professional learning of educators, poses seven "Learning Forward Professional Learning Standards":

- Learning Communities—Occurs within learning communities committed to continuous improvement, collective responsibility, and goal alignment.
- Leadership—Requires skillful leaders who develop capacity, advocate, and create support systems for professional learning.
- Resources—Requires prioritizing, monitoring, and coordinating resources for educator learning.
- Data—Uses a variety of sources and types of student, educator, and system data to plan, assess, and evaluate professional learning.
- Learning designs—Integrates theories, research, and models of human learning to achieve its intended outcomes.
- Implementation—Applies research on change and sustains support for implementation of professional learning for long-term change.
- Outcomes—Aligns its outcomes with educator performance and student curriculum standards. (Lindsey, Kearney, Estrada, Terrell, & Lindsey, 2015)

The professional learning standards are designed to provide for effective teaching practices, supportive leadership, and improved student results. The purpose of professional learning standards is for educators to develop the knowledge, skills, practices, and dispositions they need to help students perform at higher levels. Learning Forward's Overview of Standards for Professional Learning indicates that "widespread attention to the standards increases equity of access to a high-quality education for every student, not just for those lucky enough to attend schools in more advantaged communities" (Learning Forward, 2011).

We invite you to keep your journal nearby as you journey through the chapters in this book. We are confident that this mindful approach to your reading and thinking will inform your teaching and leading in ways that continue to enhance your success with our children and youth. We begin this book with a poem from our colleague Dr. Richard Gordon, professor at California State University-Dominguez Hills, California, who graciously agreed to have his poem published in our book. He found out about our book and its focus during a dinner in Rome, Italy, this past January 2016 while he was attending a conference. It captures the essence of this book. Enjoy the journey!

Along the Way

Blanca her family and their community
Traveled north—Florida to PA
Stopping and stooping
Harvesting seasonal crops
Along the way

Blanca her family and their community
Traveled to my PA university
Stopping and stooping
For mushrooms
Along the way

Blanca and community children too young
To stoop in fields for mushrooms
Traveled to my classroom
To ease their way
Along the way

Blanca and other community children
Sat, listened and danced in my classroom
Swooning on words
Traveling to imaginary places
Along the way

Blanca her family and their community
Traveled north—PA to Maine
Stopping and stooping
Harvesting seasonal crops
Along the way

Blanca her family and their community
Traveled south—Maine to PA
Stopping and stooping
Harvesting seasonal crops
Along the way

Blanca and the migrant community children
Traveled to my classroom once again
I sat and listened in a language new to me
Descriptions of life they lived
Along the way

While in PA
Blanca and her community told me
The experience of migrant worker life
Shared with me their eagerness to learn
Along the way

Blanca her family and their community
Traveled south—PA to Florida
Stopping and stooping
Harvesting seasonal crops
Along the way

Bianca her family and her community
Taught me to respect individuals
Taught me to know and respect communities
Taught me to value my time in their lives
I became a teacher
Along the way

—Richard K. Gordon

Chapter 1

Educating Children of Migrant Farmworkers

An Introduction

"We need to help students and parents cherish and preserve the ethnic and cultural diversity that nourishes and strengthens this community—and this nation."
"¡Si se puede!"

—Cesar Chavez

GETTING CENTERED

We begin by asking you to think about your role when working with students from migrant families. As a teacher, counselor, administrator, or service agency provider, undoubtedly you are aware of students who are children of farm-working families in your school and in your community. These students' academic and language proficiency in English may be below your English-speaking students. Their families may not be sure where to receive social services dedicated to migrant families.

If you are a teacher, take a moment and think about your students who are from migrant families. In the event you don't know of migrant students in your class, think of migrant students in your school. Should you be a counselor or administrator, focus on immigrants who have been identified as migrant students or families based on federal guidelines. They might be second-generation migrant students, and they may speak a form of English considered nonstandard due to their parents' ethnic and language backgrounds.

If you are a counselor or administrator, or a service agency provider, take a moment to discern your level of comfort in learning how to support teachers or personnel in learning and using new teaching or learning or social service models or approaches. You may never have had a migrant student in your

OPPORTUNITY TO JOURNAL

Turning to your journal, respond to this prompt: *In what ways do you describe your migrant students, their families, their neighborhoods, or all of them?*

classroom, and, in that case, we invite you to think about your knowledge in acquiring and using teaching or learning models or approaches in working with migrant students and their families about whom you are teaching.

OUR APPROACH

In this book, we use case stories of cultural identity exploration and discovery as a guide for you to consider yourself within the context of the classrooms, schools, and communities you serve. We describe the main traits of mobility, belonging, and anonymization that define the life stories of migrant students and their families. This book is designed for use as a professional development tool; it employs case stories in combination with reflection and dialogic techniques in the hope that it will enable you to examine prevailing practices and policies in place at your school. In the final chapter, you are encouraged to develop personal and organizational action plans aimed at initiating and institutionalizing policies and practices that will ensure migrant student access and achievement.

This book begins and ends with a focus on one's self with the premise that one cannot adequately lead change in schools or other organizations until one truly knows and understands one's self as an educator. The "Inside-Out" feature of Cultural Proficiency can be a first step in ongoing educational reform and systemic school improvement.

MIGRANT STUDENTS AS ASSETS

An influx of migrant students and families into school communities is sometimes an educational as well as a social services challenge. Even in communities that have had a long-standing contingent of migrant families and students, educational and social services challenges still exist. In this book we use the Tools of Cultural Proficiency to speak to educators who value the assets that many migrant families and their children bring from many countries.

We know that migrant students and their families have rich cultural and language backgrounds. We believe when we as educators embrace students' cultural backgrounds of language, race, gender, and socioeconomic as assets we can then construct their educational experiences into our educational programs.

The Tools of Cultural Proficiency can form a foundation for curriculum, instruction, assessment, social services, and leadership. Cultural proficiency fosters an institutionalized belief system that focuses on what students can do as opposed to deficit belief systems that concentrate on what students cannot do, thereby resulting in lowered expectations. Educators become knowledgeable about how lowered assumptions affect their values and behaviors toward migrant students and their families. Culturally proficient schools, educators, and social services personnel challenge themselves to examine deeply held assumptions that result in the current educational policies and practices that negatively impact migrant students and their families. The point of this self-examination exercise is to help these personnel develop the core values that will lower and eventually eradicate individual and systemic institutional barriers to student learning.

CHANGING DEMOGRAPHY AND OUR CLASSROOMS

If you picked up this book because of your abiding interest in serving the needs of students from migrant families, or because you are just plain curious, the data in this section may not be new to you. We review and summarize the data so that you and your colleagues can be aware that similar experiences are shared across the United States and Canada. By knowing the essence of this data, you are well prepared to respond to those who are less informed or who might be resistant to the topic of educating students from migrant families.

General approaches to multiculturalism run the risk of overlooking this increasingly diverse student population that deserves special consideration and attention—students from immigrant backgrounds whose families toil the fields in order to provide better educational opportunities for their children, many of whom are English-learning students. The enrollment of English-learning students in U.S. schools has surged in recent years. The 2012–2013 language census reported that English learners made up 9.2% of the total K–12 student enrollment, totaling 4,397,318 (USDOE, 2014). In California alone, the English-learning student enrollment for 2012–2013 was reported at over 1,391,913 million, representing 22.8% of the total student enrollment (USDOE, 2014).

Demographic shifts across our national borders are bringing increasing numbers of migrant students from diverse linguistic backgrounds into our public, religious, and private pre-K–12 schools. Providing academic and social services to migrant students and their families in our nation's schools is a need yet to be addressed adequately.

There is a paramount need in our schools for educators and associated personnel who are committed, dedicated, and sensitive to the needs of children of migrant farmworkers. Addressing the educational and support needs of children and youth from migrant families, who are among the most educationally underserved in our schools today, must be a top priority for school districts and teacher preservice and in-service programs (Bejarano & Valverde, 2012; Green, 2003; Hinkle, Tipton, 1979; Mathur, 2011; Quezada, 1991; Veaco, 1973; Vocke & Pfeiffer, 2009).

For the most part, migrant students' needs are greater than those of non-migrant students, low-income students, and ethnically different students (as well as of students who fall into one or more of those categories). According to the U.S. Department of Education (DOE), 34% of all migrant students in the United States are English Language Learners. Also, 74% of the migrant children participating in migrant education programs are enrolled in schoolwide programs and 26% were enrolled in targeted assistance programs.

The DOE documented that a contributing factor to the low performance of migrant students is school personnel having minimal or no training in meeting the specific needs of migrant students. This lack of support for migrant students is manifest in the difficult transitions students face as they move from school to school, in the lack of effective assessment tools for testing migrant students, and in the lack of programs to prepare migrant students for options beyond high school, as well as in the lack of financial resources and support for schoolwide changes (U.S. Department of Education, Migrant Education Program Annual Report: Eligibility, Participation, Services and Achievement, 2006).

Serving the educational needs of our migrant students has become a conundrum for many schools. To successfully educate migrant students, our schools must develop long-term approaches to their professional development and resist reliance on discrete short-term instructional strategies. Our experiences are that instructional strategies must be learned, coached, and applied in a context where teachers and those who support teachers share the belief that educators, teachers, and administrators can teach migrant students and that migrant students deserve high-quality instruction. Nationwide, migrant education programs can become pilot programs in which models of Cultural Proficiency are implemented, with personnel trained to work with migrant students and their families. With these beliefs and practices in place, educators are equipped to use education models appropriate to their school and community needs.

BACKGROUND, HISTORY, AND CONTEXT
OF MIGRANT EDUCATION

Legislation

The needs of migrant children and their families have been documented extensively. The Interstate Migrant Education Council noted in 1987 that migrant children's "success rate is minimal in society that has frequently left them to fend for themselves" (Interstate Migrant Education Council, 1987, p. 5). In response, the federal government reauthorized the Elementary and Secondary Education Act of 1965 to improve the education of America's children from disadvantaged backgrounds, that is, those who were identified as socioeconomically poor under federal guidelines; it also specifically addressed the children of migrant workers under Title I Part C of the legislation, which was formulated in 1966. This legislation authorized the Migrant Education Program (MEP) to provide formula grants to state education agencies for the express purpose of establishing or improving educational programs for the children of migrant workers. In the Preliminary Guidance for Title I, Part C, Public Law 103–382, the U.S. Department of Education states the following:

> The general purpose of the MEP is to ensure that children of migrant workers have access to the same free, appropriate public education, including public preschool education, provided to other children. To achieve this purpose, the MEP helps state and local education agencies remove barriers to the school enrollment, attendance, and achievement of migrant children.

The MEP is the main entity nationally for the provision of supplementary educational and related services to migrant children and their families. Their services are aligned with the accountability and performance legislation of the 1990s, particularly the Improving America's School's Act of 1994, Government Performance and Results Act of 1993, and the Public Schools Accountability Act of 1999. The MEP is aligned with accountability and performance legislation to help migrant students "at risk" of failing each state's educational content and performance standards (BCOE, 2012). Using federal migrant education funds, states are able to provide academic services, remedial and compensatory programs, bilingual and multicultural education, and counseling and preschooling (DOE, 2011).

Needs of Migrant Students and Their Families

Children are federally recognized as "migrant students" if they travel with a parent or guardian who is a seasonal worker or migrant worker with the intent to work in agriculture, fishing, forestry, and plant nursery industries. While a majority of these workers travel within the United States, a growing number of migrants are engaging in transnational migration.

The 1998 study "Farm Workers in California" finds that farmworkers have the lowest earning of any group, the highest poverty rate in the state, the second-lowest homeownership, the lowest rate of health insurance and many health problems, are overwhelmingly Latino or Mexican, and have a lower educational attainment than any other group (over 69% of agricultural workers have no high school diploma). The sons and daughters of agricultural or migrant workers fare little better than their parents. Migrant students are by far one of the least educated groups in California, with many of them not being fluent English speakers (BCOE, 2012).

The California DOE reports there are over 500,000 migrant students nationwide. In California alone, the number of migrant students enrolled in California public schools during 2012–2013 was reported to be 122,145 (CDE, 2013). In a report commissioned by the U.S. Office of Migrant Education (OME) (1998), it was reported that migrant students disproportionately attend schools classified as "high poverty" and having "larger proportion of minority students" (p. 5). Migrant students are predominantly of Latino or Mexican descent and face the same educational inadequacies, if not worse, as their urban counterparts.

In 2012, the same conditions existed. About 60% of California's school districts enrolled migrant children, 98% of whom were Latino students; less than 15% attained proficiency levels in language arts and less than 28% were proficient in math. Therefore, to change this pattern, what is needed is to engage migrant students and connect them with their school community; this would make migrant students less likely to drop out of school, thereby avoiding the prospect of another generation of low academic performance. The assumption here is that by staying in school, migrant students are much more likely to aspire to higher education and varied career paths.

OPPORTUNITY TO JOURNAL

By now you are familiar with the process of incorporating use of the journal in your professional learning through interacting with this book, so we ask you to consider this prompt: *What is the demographic profile of migrant students in your school? Where and how do you access that information? To what extent is this demographic data discussed at faculty meetings? What questions are arising for you?*

It is imperative that pre-K–12 educators are equipped to serve this population that has continued to be ignored and marginalized due to their status in society. As no one program can decrease the educational gap between migrant students and other demographic groups, it is important to introduce a variety of programs that integrate the students into the school community and help improve their academic skills (Gandara, 2011). Kozoll, Osborne, and García (2003) document that migrant students' academic success is facilitated when "teachers accept students as they are, with the language they speak at home and value systems they live within" (p. 579).

CULTURAL PROFICIENCY AND MIGRANT STUDENTS

Given the growing numbers of immigrant and migrant students in Mexico, Canada, and the United States, it is vital that educators, school districts or school boards, and social service agencies are culturally proficient and have the knowledge and skills needed to work effectively with migrant students. As educators we must believe and reaffirm these basic principles:

• Believing educators and personnel of migrant students can learn is evidence of schools moving beyond negative stereotypes and becoming Culturally Competent.
• Recognizing particular teaching and learning challenges faced by migrant students and their families is foundational for the use of basic linguistically and culturally diverse education strategies and services.
• Incorporating the language and cultural experiences of migrant students and their families into the curriculum is vital to creating culturally proficient classrooms and schools or school districts or both.

These principles are grounded in valuing the agricultural lifestyle of migrant families and embracing native languages and cultures as assets, and they are an important foundation for work with migrant students. The two sections that follow provide rich descriptions of services for migrant students and, in many cases, their families. As you read about the services, keep the three above-mentioned basic principles in the forefront of your thinking. As you do so, you will notice that the services of migrant students' cultures are being embraced as assets on which to build their educational experiences.

U.S. MIGRANT EDUCATION PROGRAMS AND SERVICES: AN OVERVIEW

Migrant students and their families receive supplemental services from the MEP in seven different areas—preschool, English-language arts, mathematics, high school graduation, out-of-school youth (OSY), health, and parent involvement. Regions and school districts develop programs that are reviewed, and approved when in compliance, by the Migrant Education Office (MEO) at the state level. All migrant programs must be supplemental to other services migrant students might receive, such as those under Title III, when migrant students are also English learners. Moreover, all programs must be aligned with the goals set by the State Service Delivery Plan (SSDP), and states should update their SSDP's every five years, as mandated by federal law (ESEA Title I, Part C).

The SSDP is a collaborative effort between the MEO and stakeholders from migrant regions, school districts, and county offices. SSDP serves as a guide for program design and development, technical assistance, and assessment of all the services and programs offered to migrant students and their families in the seven aforesaid areas. What follows is a description of each area, which includes the goals and the type of projects implemented to support migrant students between the ages of two and twenty-two years and their families.

Preschool

Services to migrant students of ages two to five years and their families are provided under the Migrant Education Even Start (MEES) program and Migrant Education School Readiness Program (MESRP). Both programs are designed to increase the [bi]literacy skills children and parents have already acquired in their daily interactions. Migrant students participate in early childhood [bi]literacy programs, and parents receive services such as adult education and parenting skills. The main goal is to equip both migrant children and their parents, with equal literacy skills as their nonmigrant peers (Rodríguez-Valls, Montoya & Valenzuela, 2014).

Projects in this area are delivered via two different pathways: home based and site based. The latter calls for migrant families coming to school sites to participate in interactive parent–child [bi]literacy activities. The former allows migrant families to receive the same type of services in their homes. Paraprofessionals meet migrant families once a week in their homes, and they work on developing bi[literacy] skills on phonemic awareness, prereading, and prewriting competencies. Both settings share a common goal, which is to reduce the age gap when entering kindergarten between migrant and nonmigrant students.

English-Language Arts

Moving from city to city or across states makes it harder for migrant students to reach achievement levels similar to their nonmigrant peers. To overcome these challenges, the MEP develops before-school, after-school, Saturday-school, and summer-school programs, in which migrant students from kindergarten to high school receive supplemental services in speaking, listening, reading, and writing skills. Projects in this area include writing workshops, speech and debate activities, and test-taking skills. The main goal, especially after the Common Core Standards has come into place, is to ensure migrant students are not left behind (Rodríguez-Valls, Kofford & Morales, 2012).

Mathematics

Math programs for migrant students are frequently combined with the supplemental programs of English-language arts. The focus in the context of mathematics is to build capacity among migrant students to distinguish and comprehend the role mathematics plays in their world, as well as to be able to reason based on evidence. Math programs and English-language arts always include a parent component where migrant parents develop awareness on the challenges their children face at school and the concepts migrant children learn in algebra, calculus, and geometry.

High School Graduation

Increasing the high school graduation rate is a shared goal of all the SSDPs nationwide. Lundy-Ponce (2010) reports that the dropout rates among migrant high school students range between 45% and 65%. In California, projects attempting to reduce the dropout rates concentrate on building the skills needed to pass the California High School Exit Exam. Overall, programs are developed to prepare migrant students for college and for any professional pathway they would like to pursue after they graduate from high school.

Out-of-School Youth

Working with migrant students aged between sixteen and twenty-two has always been one of the top challenges for the MEP. Identifying and recruiting students within this age range requires time; but, most importantly, there is a need to build confianza [trust] among a wary population that is always alert for the outcomes of the immigration dialogue ongoing between the United States, Canada, and Mexico (Patel, 2012; Rodríguez-Valls & Torres, 2014; Suarez-Orozco, Suarez-Orozco & Todorova, 2010).

There are two unique OSY groups: (a) high school dropouts and (b) migrant youth who come to the United States to work in the fields,

cannery industry, or in slaughterhouses. With both groups, projects target four different topics: (a) referral to English as a Second Language,
General Education Development, or vocational courses (or all of them);
(b) educational counseling; (c) transportation; and (d) medical or dental
appointments.

Health

The MEP is unique because of the uniqueness—the constant traveling in
pursuit of agricultural jobs—of migrant families. These jobs expose parents
and their children to hazardous settings. Therefore, the services provided
by the MEP go beyond educational needs. These services support families
with basic medical, dental, and vision care, and provide referrals to other
medical treatments. Thus, projects in this area attempt to be proactive and
preventive—they educate migrant families on topics such as obesity, stress,
domestic violence, and pesticides, among others. The goal, like in the other
areas, is to build competence that is capable of being sustained and extended
well after families are no longer eligible for migrant services.

Parent Involvement

Educating migrant parents is the core of all services provided by the MEP.
Parents constitute local, regional, and state advisory councils. Their role is to
provide advice to the superintendent of schools on the needs of migrant students and parents. Historically, migrant parents have been at the forefront by
asking for better job conditions in the field and requesting additional support
and funding for MEPs.

Projects in this area follow a training of trainers model, in line with which
local, regional, and state migrant representatives first acquire knowledge
and then transfer it to their peers within the school district, county office,
and state. The majority of states host an annual parent conference in which
migrant parents convene to share experiences and concerns, as well as to participate in workshops aligned with the objectives set by the SSDP.

OPPORTUNITY TO JOURNAL

Once again, turning to your journal consider this prompt: *In what ways did
this section add to your knowledge about services for migrant students?
In what ways did it affirm what you already knew?*

SUPPORTS FOR MIGRANT STUDENTS

Apart from the seven areas described above, the MEP includes other student support projects in which students obtain tools to accomplish their dreams and to secure their academic success and achievement. These programs include tutorial services, support when migrant students are enrolled in their undergraduate studies, and reinforcing high school graduation, as well as promoting leadership roles. The next five programs are established in some states across the United States. All of them are funded by competitive grants offered by the OME in Washington, DC, or, like the California Mini-Corps Program and Migrant Summer Leadership Institutes (MSLI), which are funded by the statewide operations MEP budget, in this case California's.

CAMP

The College Assistance Migrant Program (CAMP) provides counseling, tutoring, and support in other areas to migrant students in their first year of undergraduate studies at an institution of higher education (as described on the OME's website).

HEP

The High School Equivalency Program (HEP) is an extension of the aforesaid high school and OSY services. HEP helps migrant students aged 16 or older to gain what corresponds to a high school diploma and afterward to find a job, or to enter a postsecondary education, or to begin professional training (as described on the OME's website).

Binational Migrant Education Program

A number of migrant students travel back and forth every year from Mexico to the United States. To support and enrich their stay in the United States, teachers from Mexico participate in six- to eight-week summer programs in which they share the culture and customs of these students with the more permanent migrant students. Teachers also learn how the educational system works in the United States; hence, they are better prepared when the migrant students come back to Mexico by being knowledgeable of each state's educational system.

California Mini-Corps

This program is designed to reinforce the work K–12 migrant students are completing in their schools. Working under the supervision of the classroom teacher, tutors provide support to migrant students in various subject areas—for example, mathematics, language arts, science, and social studies. The majority of these tutors come from a migrant family background, thus they are relevant role models for the new generations of K–12 migrant students.

Migrant Summer Leadership Institutes

Freshmen and junior high school students in California participate in summer institutes, whose focus for the last three years has been science, technology, engineering, and mathematics. MSLI are a two-week residential, academic program hosted by Cal State or UC universities. The goal is to prepare students for an easy transition to postsecondary education.

OPPORTUNITY TO JOURNAL

As you now know, there are extensive services that provide ongoing support for migrant students. Turning to your journal: What questions do you have about how well this information is known in your school and about the migrant community served by your school?

PROFESSIONAL LEARNING IN SUPPORT OF MIGRANT STUDENTS

Working with and for migrant families requires a specific set of skills to maximize the effectiveness of the supplemental programs described above. In this section, we explore cultural proficiency as it applies in terms of understanding the assets—cultural, linguistic, and social capital—migrant students bring to their schools, school districts, and counties. As we prepare educators to be able to work with and learn from migrant families, they must learn to approach migrant students and their families with an additive, asset-based approach rather than a subtractive, deficit-based educational framework (Valenzuela, 1999).

Migrant families possess valuable funds of knowledge that educators and staff must use when developing effective programs. The key for educator professional learning programs is to fully understand the challenges and struggles migrant families experience due to their frequent movement from one city or town to another. All personnel working with such families—teachers, paraprofessionals, administrators, and staff—can develop high levels of cultural proficiency and understanding of the realities faced by these families through reflecting on their own values and behaviors and their school's policies and practices.

Cross (1989) in his seminal work described the process of becoming cultural proficient as an inside-out process. You will repeatedly come across the term inside-out process in this book. It is a key concept because it holds that the learning begins with us as educators—after all, we are best placed to understand our assumptions. We can retain those assumptions that are productive and expel those that impede our ability to be effective when working with migrant communities. Professional learning must begin by building critical awareness on two key concepts: anonymization and lack of belonging, which migrant families experience when arriving in a new city.

Personnel should seek to build the confianza[trust] of newly arrived migrant families. Mutual respect, care, and commitment are needed before migrant parents are ready, and willing, to participate in all the services and projects described in the previous section. Each person working with migrant families must question what he or she knows about the two key concepts and how these can be incorporated and further analyzed in each migrant project. There is an unlearning process in which some myths—such as migrant and immigrant students are the same, all migrant students are English learners, and all migrant families speak Spanish—need to be revised and unraveled.

With this book we use the lens of Cultural Proficiency to focus on the theoretical and praxial knowledge needed by educators to inform us of the importance of how anonymization, sense of belonging, and mobility influence the learning outcomes of migrant projects, the successful achievement of migrant students, and the empowerment of migrant parents. We believe culturally proficient migrant regions, school districts, and county offices must ignite the energy needed to provide high-quality, effective programs that will help migrant students and their families to become a recognizable student population in the communities where they belong, despite their propensity to move from one town to another. As Patel (2012) states, "We must resist facile comfort that because different populations might be included in some aspects of a society, therefore meaningful, comprehensive, and just inclusion in society's structures is happening" (p. 1).We extend the idea of inclusion to ensure migrant programs build bridges that migrant students and their families can cross toward achieving their dreams, within a society where they can work with, and learn from, all their neighbors.

GOING DEEPER

Take a moment and review your entries under the Getting Centered prompt at the opening of this chapter and the Opportunities to Journal sections throughout each chapter where you will be able to reflect on your personal thoughts on the readings and content. Having read about plight of migrant students and their families as well as the services available through the national Migrant Education Program that shapes international, national, state, and local policies, in what ways are you more informed in serving the migrant students in your classroom, school, or the community you serve? What are your goals as you continue reading this book? Please use your journal to record your thinking.

Dialogic Activity

Though this activity is intended to promote dialogic conversations with and among your colleagues, you may want to use your journal to organize your own thinking. As you consider your school and the diverse community you serve, what are some topics from this chapter that suggest questions you want to keep in front of you as you read and discuss subsequent chapters? In what ways does your school or district appropriately provide services for migrant students and their families? What questions does this chapter raise for you?

Chapter 2 presents the conceptual framework for the Tools of Cultural Proficiency. The chapter describes and guides you through consideration of each of the Tools of Cultural Proficiency. In this chapter, the focus will be on Tools of Cultural Proficiency within the context of migrant students, their families, their educators, and social service personnel. You will be engaged with questions for reflection and dialogue to enrich your understanding of the use of Tools for Cultural Proficiency and use of the tools with your school's change initiatives. The tools provide you with a framework for examining your own values and behaviors and the policies and practices of, your school, or your social service agency. More importantly, the tools will support your continuing professional learning as an educator in effectively serving all students in your school.

Chapter 2

The Tools of Cultural
Proficiency for Educator Use

Deficit perspectives on the abilities of minority group communities in
the wider society are frequently communicated directly or indirectly
to students in teacher-student interactions.

—Jim Cummins (2013, p. 16)

GETTING CENTERED

"Equity" and "access" have emerged as important words in the discussion on twenty-first-century education. If these words are to stop becoming "buzzwords" with no real-world implications for students, we believe it is important to ensure that we have standard definitions of these words. Take a moment to explore your current thinking about these two important concepts.

OPPORTUNITY TO JOURNAL

Returning to your journal, take a few moments and write your definition of *equity* and *access* (Okay, you are on the honor system now! No using online search tools!). For this activity to be meaningful, it is important to probe your own understanding. It is okay if you struggle with this; you don't have to share your work with anyone!

This chapter presents the Tools of Cultural Proficiency, which are grounded in the ethical principle that schools must be places that are as welcoming to migrant children and youth as they are to other students. This notion is in line with chapter 1, where we introduced the *inside-out approach* for educators, which if adopted could ensure that our schools are places where all students are equally embraced, with their varied cultural norms and values and given due respect. As you proceed through this book, you will learn that our work as educators has at its core a strong commitment to equity and access; to us, equity and access, in the context of teaching, means learning how to have productive relationships with all students, but especially with students from migrant families.

FROM WHY? TO INSIDE-OUT

The policies and practices of educators as well as district authorities reflect the value they attach to ensuring equitable outcomes for all students, regardless of the students' values, and beliefs (Terrell & Lindsey, 2009).

Traditionally, procedural questions have dominated discussions about curriculum, instruction, accountability, and assessment. Here are some of them:

- What are the curricular units to be covered this year?
- What are the steps to accomplishing our goal?
- How do we implement differentiation in heterogeneous classrooms?

Educators are and will always be faced with these and many other important and relevant procedural questions that will always be with us. However, when considering equity and access issues, the most important question may not begin with *What* or *How*, but with *Why*.

Sinek (2009) has taught us to ask the important *why* questions and not to get mired in the energy-consuming *what* and *how* questions. Culturally proficient educators are guided by *why* questions intended to constructively inform the district and its schools. Here are some relevant questions:

- Why do achievement gaps persist between migrant students and other students, including English-learning students who are not from migrant families?
- Why are migrant students overrepresented in special education?
- Why are migrant students underrepresented in honors and advanced placement courses and in international baccalaureate programs?
- Why are the rates of absenteeism of migrant students so much higher than other students?

- Why do migrant students drop out of school at rates much higher than other ethnic or cultural groups of students?

Pause for a moment and think about the distinctions between the *how, what,* and *why* questions. We intend to challenge, inform, and, in some cases, modify your current thinking, as you learn more about the Tools of Cultural Proficiency. In chapters 5–9, you will see how the Tools of Cultural Proficiency can be applied while working with students from migrant families. It is going to be an exciting journey because it is likely to take you further along the path of self-discovery and to provide you with insights that may lead to you become a consistently effective educator.

YOUTUBE MOMENT

Take a five-minute break and, using whatever technology you have at hand, access this video on YouTube—Simon Sinek's *Start with Why* (at https://www.youtube.com/watch?v=IPYeCltXpxw). This video will help you deepen your understanding of the inside-out approach and thereby to become a culturally proficient educator. Once your interest is piqued with this brief Sinek video, you will be ready to view his full eighteen-minute TED talk, at //www.youtube.com/watch?v=sioZd3AxmnE. (The video is also available on the TED website—How Great Leaders Inspire Action, at http://www.ted.com/talks/simon_sinek_how_great_leaders_inspire_action.)

Don't get hung up on the word "leader." Whether your educational role is that of teacher, counselor, administrator, or paraprofessional, you are a leader to your students and their families in providing equitable educational opportunities. Asking "why" questions in addition to the more procedural "what" and "how" questions will provide you with an opportunity to examine the extent to which your espoused values align with your behavior—in other words, to ask yourself: *is what you say what you do?* Once you begin introspecting, it is important to also examine your school's policies and practices and ensure that they align with the needs of the students currently enrolled in your school, as opposed to the students who used to attend your school or the students you wish went to your school.

As previously indicated, Cross (1989), in his groundbreaking work on cultural competence, identified this sense of openness to curiosity as an inside-out process basic to educators' personal and professional growth and to schools' institutional change. At both the personal and institutional levels, reflection and dialogue are communication skills that facilitate the inside-out process of change.

- For individual educators, reflection is the "communication skill" used to probe and uncover deeply held assumptions about their students; in this book, educators' assumptions about students from migrant communities are examined.
- At the institutional level of schools and their districts, educators engaged in authentic dialogue can probe the assumptions embedded in prevailing policies and practices and the extent to which these assumptions may, consciously or unconsciously, devalue the cultures of migrant families, thereby fostering access and achievement disparities.

Our experiences indicate that policies and practices do not intentionally target migrant students for discriminatory treatment; rather, seemingly innocuous policies and practices too often render invisible the assets these students bring to school. Migrant students become marginalized due to prevailing policies and practices devised to serve the needs of other, often mainstream, demographic groups of students. As an example, migrant students and their families, in the first weeks of their arrival to a new school district, often experience a sense of anonymization.

Migrant students encounter new classmates, teachers, and administrators, and their parents attempt to navigate a new educational network. Educators sometimes have misconceptions of migrant students as they are labeled immigrant students or English-learning students or both. These misconceptions and the lack of awareness on the unique nature of migratory families prevent them from receiving the required supplemental services (i.e., afterschool programs, medical referrals, and tutorials) that could help them to overcome the aforesaid anonymization and, most importantly, to develop a sense of belonging within their new community.

In stark contrast, culturally proficient educators are mindfully guided by a deeply held belief that their students deserve high-quality education and that they and their colleagues are capable of learning how to educate all their students—in particular the migrant students. Family Biliteracy Project (FBP) and the Migrant Summer Academies (MSA) are examples of high-quality programs operated by culturally proficient educators. MSA are designed to enrich migrant students' learning processes with a nontraditional, student-centered curriculum that esteems communication between teachers and students.

FBP promotes the idea of the whole family working together to enhance, enrich, and increase the funds of knowledge and literacies they carry as they move from city to city. Both initiatives, FBP and MSA, were built following Hooks' (2010) concept of engaged pedagogy, which "establishes a mutual relationship between teacher and [migrant] students that nurtures the growth of both parties, creating an atmosphere of trust and commitment" (p. 22).

OPPORTUNITY TO JOURNAL

This is an opportune time to pause and consider Sinek's parsing of the *what*, *how* and *why* questions along with Cross's *inside-out* approach to individual and institutional change. Using your journal, take a few moments and record your thinking, your feelings and reactions to the material, and/or questions that may be surfacing for you.

THE TOOLS OF CULTURAL PROFICIENCY

The Tools of Cultural Proficiency are a powerful set of four interrelated tools that enable educators to respond effectively in cross-cultural environments and guide personal and organizational changes (Lindsey, Nuri Robins & Terrell, 2009). These tools are presented in integrated fashion in Figure 2.1.

The Tools of Cultural Proficiency are:

- Recognizing and acknowledging barriers to cultural proficiency:
  ○ Systems of oppression
  ○ The presumption of entitlement and privilege
  ○ Unawareness of the need to adapt
  ○ Resistance to change
- The Guiding Principles of Cultural Proficiency:
  ○ Culture is a predominant force; you cannot not have culture.
  ○ People are served in varying degrees by the dominant culture.
  ○ The group identity of individuals is as important as their individual identities.
  ○ Diversity within cultures is vast and significant.
  ○ Each group has unique cultural needs.
  ○ The family, as defined by each culture, is the primary system of support in the education of children.
  ○ Marginalized populations have to be at least bicultural, and this creates a distinct set of issues to which the system must be equipped to respond.
  ○ Inherent in cross-cultural interactions are dynamics that must be acknowledged, adjusted to, and accepted.
  ○ The school system must incorporate cultural knowledge into practice and policy making.
- Six points of values, behaviors, policies, and practices along the continuum:
  ○ Informed by the barriers:
    ○ Cultural destructiveness
    ○ Cultural incapacity

The Five Essential Elements of Cultural Competence

Serve as standards for personal, professional values and behaviors, as well as organizational policies and practices:

- Assessing cultural knowledge
- Valuing diversity
- Managing the dynamics of difference
- Adapting to diversity
- Institutionalizing cultural knowledge

Informs

The Cultural Proficiency Continuum portrays people and organizations who possess the knowledge, skills, and moral bearing to distinguish among healthy and unhealthy practices as represented by different worldviews:

Unhealthy Practices:

- Cultural destructiveness
- Cultural incapacity
- Cultural blindness

Differing Worldviews

Healthy Practices:

- Cultural precompetence
- Cultural competence
- Cultural proficiency

Informs

Informs

Resolving the tension to do what is socially just within our diverse society leads people and organizations to view selves in terms Unhealthy and Healthy.

Barriers to Cultural Proficiency

Serve as personal, professional, and institutional impediments to moral and just service to a diverse society by

- being resistant to change,
- being unaware of the need to adapt,
- not acknowledging systemic oppression, and
- benefiting from a sense of privilege and entitlement.

E
t
h
i
c
a
l
T
e
n
s
i
o
n

Guiding Principles of Cultural Proficiency

Provide a moral framework for conducting one's self and organization in an ethical fashion by believing the following:

- Culture is a predominant force in society.
- People are served in varying degrees by the dominant culture.
- People have individual and group identities.
- Diversity within cultures is vast and significant.
- Each cultural group has unique cultural needs.
- The best of both worlds enhances the capacity of all.
- The family, as defined by each culture, is the primary system of support in the education of children.
- School systems must recognize that marginalized populations have to be at least bicultural and that this status creates a distinct set of issues to which the system must be equipped to respond.
- Inherent in cross-cultural interactions are dynamics that must be acknowledged, adjusted to, and accepted.

Figure 2.1   The Conceptual Framework of Cultural Proficiency. *Source*: Randall, B. Lindsey, Kikanza Nuri Robins, and Raymond D. Terrell. *Cultural Proficiency: A Manual for School Leaders* (3rd Edition) (Thousand Oaks, CA: Corwin Press, 2009).

- ₒ Cultural blindness
- ₒ Informed by the guiding principles:
- ₒ Cultural precompetence
- ₒ Cultural competence
- ₒ Cultural proficiency
- The essential elements as standards of culturally competent values, behaviors, policies, and practices:
  - ₒ Assessing cultural knowledge
  - ₒ Valuing diversity
  - ₒ Managing the dynamics of difference
  - ₒ Adapting to diversity
  - ₒ Institutionalizing cultural knowledge (Cross, 1989; Lindsey, Nuri Robins, and Terrell, 2009)

THE PURPOSE AND FUNCTION OF THE TOOLS

We exist in a world in which these tools cannot exist in isolation from one another. They are presented above independently only for the purpose of introducing and briefly describing them. In this section, we will describe the tools in the context of individual and institutional realities. Chapter 4 presents a rubric to demonstrate how the tools act together and the way in which they illustrate the range of experiences—both negative and positive—that students from migrant families may have in our schools.

Overcoming Barriers

The barriers denote individual, institutional, and systemic impediments to change. Individuals should understand the extent to which various "isms" may be present in their behaviors as well as in their school's policies and practices. This can be a difficult process for some people as they might believe they are being blamed for the existence of what are systemic "isms."

When educators introspect in order to understand how the various "isms" impact their behavior, they come to realize that they, like students and their parents, are not personally responsible for the circumstances that foster inequities. However, once confronted with the reality of the "isms," educators begin to realize that though they may not have created the values, beliefs, policies, and practices that foster the "isms," it is their responsibility to address the "isms" that impact the education of all students.

The introspection allows educators to begin to gauge students' capacity to learn as well as their own capacity to learn how to educate. This process leads to a readiness to explore the core values that support student academic learning and the professional learning of the educators. The Guiding Principles of Cultural Proficiency are the core values that enable us to confront and overcome individual and institutional barriers.

The Guiding Principles

Our experience has been that the guiding principles posed as reflective questions can guide the development of core values that entail access and equity for all students. Educators often use these questions to host dialogue sessions in their schools, which are intended to foster development of all-encompassing core values. Core values that are mindfully developed become a foundation for developing meaningful vision and mission statements that would help in guiding policy formulation and inclusive practices throughout the school. Some guiding principles are as follows:

• To what extent do you honor culture as a natural and normal part of the community you serve?
• To what extent do you recognize and understand the differential and historical treatment accorded to migrant students and their communities in our schools and communities?
• When working with migrant students and their families, to what extent do you see the person both as an individual and as a member of a group?
• To what extent do you recognize and value the differences within the migrant communities you serve?
• To what extent do you know and respect the unique needs of migrant families in the communities you serve?
• To what extent do you know how migrant families in your community define family and the manner in which family serves as the primary system of support for the students (young members) of the community?
• To what extent do you recognize your role in acknowledging, adjusting to, and accepting cross-cultural interactions a necessary social and communications dynamics?
• To what extent do you recognize and understand the bicultural reality for migrant groups historically not well served in our schools and societies?
• To what extent do you incorporate cultural knowledge into the policies, practices, and procedures of your organization (Lindsey, Terrell, Nuri Robins and Lindsey, 2009).

The Continuum

The continuum provides the educators and their schools a range of terms to use for identifying and overcoming the barriers of nonproductive policies, practices, and individual behaviors and for replacing the barriers with core values that produce socially just educational practices. Culturally proficient educators mindfully and intentionally engage in their own professional learning so as to develop communication skills that would enable them to better offer equitable learning opportunities for students from migrant families. The aforementioned six points of the continuum describe a range of unhealthy to healthy practices for educators that serve as benchmarks to locate current practices in serving students from migratory families and to inform future educational possibilities as a choice that result in full access and academic success in our schools.

The Essential Elements

The Essential Elements serve as behavioral standards for educators, enabling them to become culturally competent in their work with migrant students. The Essential Elements are assessing cultural knowledge, valuing diversity, managing the dynamics of difference, adapting to diversity, and institutionalizing cultural knowledge. Whereas the guiding principles are intended to inform the development of inclusive and equitable core values, the essential elements are "where the action is." These elements are expressed using strong verbs to guide the educators in crafting educational experiences that regard students' cultures as assets, not as deficits to be fixed or changed.

GOING DEEPER

This chapter provided an introduction to the Tools of Cultural Proficiency and an opportunity for you to reflect on your thinking and practices.

Reflective Activity

Turning to your journal, note in what ways this chapter has informed your desire to understand and recognize the importance of thinking of cultures of migrant communities as assets for the school community rather than as deficits and problems to be solved. Please use your journal to record your thinking about the tools.

Dialogic Activity

Think deeply about this prompt and, when ready, engage in in-depth discussion with colleagues for the purpose of exploring one another's thinking in a nonjudgmental manner. Keep in mind that this dialogue is for you to understand one another in ways that will enable you to provide improved opportunities for migrant children and youth. *In what ways does this chapter inform your thinking about the barriers and supports that might exist in your school that either impede or support access opportunities for children and youth from migrant families?*

We invite you to join us on our journey toward attaining culturally proficient educator practices. Chapter 3 presents examples of cultural competence, describes professional community learning, and makes a case for you and your colleagues to be leaders of learning, albeit often in nonformal ways. In chapters 5–9, we portray descriptions called "vignettes." The goal of these vignettes is to provide real-life scenarios that will aid you in becoming an "evaluator." We will ask you to reflect and engage in a dialogue on these vignettes and to create an action plan, which will build a bridge toward cultural proficiency when working with and in migrant education programs. You are to use the rubric on Cultural Proficiency as a tool to reflect on the aforesaid vignettes and to examine how this reflection will transform your own practices.

ESPERANZA COUNTY AND PRÓXIMA ESTACIÓN SCHOOL DISTRICT: A CASE STORY

In Esperanza County, a process has been going on to evaluate the county's practices when serving Priority for Service (PF) students. The core of this case story is framed within the concept of cultural competence as a tool that will help educators to design, develop and implement programs, thereby meeting the needs of PF students and their families.

Esperanza County has a student population of 30,000, out of which 35% (10,500) are migrants. The migrant population speaks five different languages: Mixteco, Punjabi, Zapoteco, Triqui, and Hmong. Out of the 10,500 students, 3,000 are PF students and 2,000 are those who qualify for preschool services. Within Esperanza County, there is Próxima Estación School District. The school district has a student population of 7,000, out of which 40% (2,800) are migrants who speak two languages, Mixteco and Zapoteco. Out of the 2,800 migrant students, 800 are PF students.

The county office and the school district have been working together to optimize the services provided to migrant students and their families. Their cooperative work is a model of effective partnership built to ensure all migrant students and their families are participating, being educated, and empowered by best practices specifically designed for migrant students.

Esperanza County:

- County Office:
  1. Dr. Antonio Ceballos, County Assistant Superintendent Educational Services
  2. Mr. Pablo Perez, Migrant Education Regional Director
  3. Ms. Mayda Marti, County Migrant Education Program Coordinator
  4. Mr. Guillermo Mayoral, County Identification Recruiter (IR) Coordinator
  5. Ms. Isela Peralta, County Identification Recruiter (IR)

Próxima Estación School District:

1. Mr. Tamarit, District Migrant Education Program Educational Services Director
2. Ms. Montoya, Teacher
3. Mr. Gutierrez, Teacher
4. Mr. Garmendia, Teacher
5. Ms. Ponce, Parent Advisory Council (PAC) and Regional Advisory Council (RAC) representative

Comprehensive Needs Assessment (CNA) team:

1. Dr. Castells, Principal Investigator (PI) of Comprehensive Needs Assessment (CNA)
2. Darren Faulkner, RA of CNA

Learning Communities + Culturally Proficient Leadership = Students from Migrant Families Being Well Served

A word as to the education of the heart. We don't believe that this can be imparted through books; it can only be imparted through the loving touch of the teacher.

—Cesar Chavez

GETTING CENTERED ACTIVITY

In the last few years, the language of professional learning communities (PLCs) has become commonplace in our profession. So, chances are quite good that you are familiar with PLCs—the concepts associated with them and the intent behind their formation. In some schools, PLC has become a new label applied to what were called grade-level or department meetings—in other words, new label on old wine. However, Hord and Sommers (2008) would argue that PLCs are new wine in new bottles—that is, they have characteristics that differentiate them from traditional grade-level or department meetings.

OPPORTUNITY TO JOURNAL

Returning to your journal, describe either your understanding of the characteristics of PLCs or describe in what ways PLCs are differentiated from regular grade-level or department meetings.

Given the growing numbers of immigrant and migrant students in Mexico, Canada, and the United States, it is vital that educators and school districts (or school boards) become more culturally proficient. Effective multicultural and culturally proficient education reaffirms these basic principles:

- Educators of students from migratory families believing they, the educators, can learn is evidence of schools moving beyond negative stereotypes to becoming culturally competent or proficient
- Educators recognizing the particular teaching and learning challenges faced by migrant students are foundational for the use of basic multicultural education strategies
- Educators incorporating the language and cultural experiences of migrant students into the curriculum are vital to creating culturally proficient classrooms, schools, and/or school districts

These principles are grounded in valuing the agricultural and urban factory lifestyles of migrant families, in embracing migratory families' native languages and cultures as assets, and in holding these principles as important foundation for work with students from migrant families and communities.

This chapter is designed to demonstrate how PLCs and culturally proficient leadership tools are well suited to serve educators and schools striving to better serve the educational needs of children whose families are migratory workers. In serving the needs of these students, schools have the opportunity to experience new things:

- Deeper professional learning about this too often overlooked cultural group of students
- Learning how to ensure that schools are inclusive of all students
- Experiencing the varied talents of nonformal leaders that may emerge from faculty and staff members

FROM PROFESSIONAL DEVELOPMENT TO PROFESSIONAL LEARNING

Whether you are a first-year teacher or a highly experienced veteran teacher, counselor, or administrator, you know intuitively that the education of our children and youth is both a formal and informal process that begins in the home and community and continues through many years of formalized learning in schools. With that in mind, this book, in particular this chapter, is devoted to your professional learning as an educator in service of students from migrant families and communities, who often attend schools in which the diversity they bring to school is overlooked and, thereby, not valued.

Learning Forward (formerly the National Staff Development Council), a foremost and well-respected source of professional learning opportunities for pre-K–12 educators, has recognized that passive sit-and-get professional development serves neither educators nor their students, who are the intended beneficiaries of educators' participation in professional development sessions. In 2011, Learning Forward published a set of standards for professional learning that has led to a shift in thinking among educators seeking to serve all students equitably—*from* viewing themselves as passive recipients of learning designed and delivered for them *to* seeing themselves as being actively involved in their own learning.

The new professional learning standards provide guidance that are focused on learning communities, leadership, resources, data, learning designs, implementation, and outcomes. The complete description of standards for professional learning is given in Resources in Support of Migrant Education. Therefore, in this chapter, we focus on the standards for learning communities. These Professional Learning Communities can increase educator effectiveness and the results for all students occurs within learning communities committed to continuous improvement, collective responsibility, and goal alignment (Lindsey, Lindsey, Hord, & Von Frank, 2015).

OPPORTUNITY TO JOURNAL

We'll make this a quick entry! In thinking about students from migrant families, what are some questions you would like for you and your school to explore, which when answered might lead to your instructional improvement, your school's collective responsibility, and you and your school attaining the goals you have for all of your students?

CULTURALLY PROFICIENT SCHOOL FUNCTIONS

With these new "Opportunity to Journal" questions fresh in your thinking, you are well prepared to build on your learning from chapter 2 and to focus on the cultural proficiency tool that is action oriented, the Essential Elements of Cultural Competence. This tool provides five standards to guide our practice as educators, as well as for our schools as learning communities. In using these five standards to guide our practices, we are shifting our PLC language—*professional learning communities* becomes *professional communities learning*.

Table 3.1 Key School Functions Aligned with the Five Essential Elements of Cultural Competence

Five Essential Elements	Curriculum and Instruction	Assessment	Parents and Community	Professional Development
		Culturally Competent Key Functions		
Valuing Diversity	Extent to which curriculum reflects diversity	Extent to which cultural differences are used to gather data	Extent to which parent and community diversity is valued	Extent to which professional learning addresses cultural issues
Assessing Culture	Extent to which opportunities are provided for educators and students to learn about themselves and others	Extent to which disaggregated data are used to enhance knowledge and shape practice	Extent to which community involvement facilitates the identification, assessment, and development of cultural identity	Extent to which professional learning addresses issues of cultural identity
Managing the Dynamics of Difference	Extent to which curriculum promotes multiple perspectives	Extent to which data is used to address the gaps between cultural groups	Extent to which community involvement efforts develop the capacity to mediate cultural conflict between and among diverse parent or community groups and the school	Extent to which professional learning promotes and models the use of inquiry and dialogue related to multiple perspectives and issues arising from diversity
Adapting to Diversity	Extent to which cultural knowledge is integrated into the curriculum	Extent to which assessments are changed to meet the needs of cultural groups	Extent to which people and schools change to meet the needs of the community	The extent to which professional learning facilitates change to meet the needs of the community
Institutionalizing	Extent to which values and policies support culturally —responsive curriculum	Extent to which assessment data shapes values and policies to meet the needs of cultural groups	Extent to which people and schools integrate knowledge about diverse community and organizational cultures into daily practice	The extent to which professional learning shapes policies and practices that meet the needs of a diverse community

Source: Used with permission from Randall B. Lindsey, Stephanie M. Graham, R. Chris Westphal, Jr., & Cynthia L. Jew. (2008). *Culturally proficient inquiry: A lens for identifying and examining educational gaps.* Thousand Oaks, CA: Corwin Press.

OPPORTUNITY TO JOURNAL

Pause for a few moments to examine the information in Table 3.1, and return to your journal to consider these questions: As you read the Culturally Competent Key Functions, what distinguishes these examples for you? What is your understanding of Professional Communities Learning? In what ways does information in Table 3.1 speak to you? As you prepare to continue your reading in this book, what questions are surfacing as you continue your learning? Take a few moments and record your responses to these questions, as well as recording other thoughts and questions that you may have.

This is not an inconsequential realignment of words. The latter construction holds professional learning as a central function of our role as educators.

Table 3.1 displays the alignment of the Essential Elements of Cultural Competence with four key school functions—curriculum and instruction, assessment, parents and community, and professional development. This alignment is done in ways to inform educators' professional learning for working more intentionally with migrant communities (adapted from Lindsey, Jungwirth, Pahl, and Lindsey, 2009).

The information in Table 3.1 begins a journey that cumulatively presents the rubric in chapter 4 and then the vignettes in chapters 5 through 9 for you to apply to your own classroom, grade level, department, or school.

- With this information about the manner in which these key school functions intersect with the Essential Elements of Cultural Competence, you will be able to use the rubric in chapter 4, Educators' Rubric for Inclusion and Support of Migrant Education Students, their Families and their Communities, as an informal assessment and planning tool for you as an individual educator and for your school learning communities.
- Chapters 5 through 9 are organized to deepen your learning with each of the essential elements and the manner in which they apply to you and your school setting(s).

PLCs are situations where leadership emerges in natural, nonforced ways. When considering professional settings where issues of diversity, equity, and inclusion are embraced as lenses through which we view the four key school functions, it may be that new voices of leadership, or authority, emerge and contribute to the group's continuous improvement.

CULTURALLY PROFICIENT LEADERSHIP
AND THE FOUR SCHOOL FUNCTIONS

Schools have formal leaders with role titles such as principal, assistant principal, lead teacher, and department chair. Of course, most any experienced educator also knows the power and value of nonformal leaders. These nonformal leaders are colleagues among us. The words of the 1970s and 1980s E. F. Hutton television commercial might be adapted, *when this or that person speaks, everyone listens.* These colleagues have our attention, and often our respect, due to longevity in the school, their specialized expertise, and, sometimes, just because of force of personality.

The point being made here is you too can be a nonformal leader in your school, and, in particular, you can be a leading voice for students from migrant families and communities. PLCs are best served by participants who are guided by curiosity and who pose questions such as: "Why does this approach work?" or "what are other approaches we might take?" Curiosity is no different when exploring more effective ways of serving the needs of students from diverse cultural groups.

In chapter 2, we described that effective school leaders know how to pose questions to guide their own and their colleagues' actions. Sinek (2009) describes the relationship among three key leadership questions:

- *What?*
- *How?*
- *Why?*

As educators we have become complacent, maybe due to the pressures of the accountability movements of recent years, into restricting ourselves to the mechanistic *What* and *How* type of questions about considering and implementing externally imposed programs and processes.

Framing questions by using all the three types can lead to understanding the too often unrecognized power of unexamined assumptions. Skillful use of these questions is fundamental to developing culturally proficient leadership. Each of the questions has a specific position of importance to reflective and dialogic processes:

- *What?*—this question identifies the result to be accomplished.
- *How?*—this question yields the process to attain the desired result.
- *Why?*—this question reveals your purpose, that is, the cause for which you are working.

Sinek's Golden Circle Model (2009) of *what, how*, and *why* questions aids us in mindfully taking the Tools of Cultural Proficiency into our actions, both as individual educators and as schools. As you will recall from chapter 2, these tools are presented independently but are interdependent in use. Effective use of the tools helps us distinguish our and our colleagues' deficit-based thinking and actions from our asset-based thinking. Far too often, deficit-based values and approaches are so deeply embedded in our practices that they often seem to be harmless actions. For your quick review, these tools are handy guides to understanding our own values and behaviors and in questioning the assumptions implied in our schools' and districts' customary policies and practices:

- Recognizing, acknowledging, and overcoming barriers to cultural proficiency
- Embracing the Guiding Principles of Cultural Proficiency to inform our core values
- Using the cultural proficiency continuum to know where we are in our journey
- Using the Essential Elements of Cultural Competence/Proficiency as a template for professional and institutional learning (Arriaga & Lindsey, 2016)

In merging Sinek's Golden Circle Model with the Tools of Cultural Proficiency, there are three distinct cycles to inform our leadership actions. Take a moment to refer to Figure 3.1. Note the manner in which equity and access guide actions for individuals and their institutions:

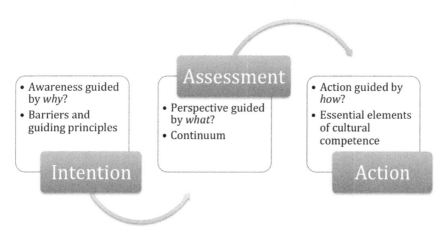

Figure 3.1   Cycles of Interrelatedness: Culturally Proficient Leadership. *Source*: Used with permission from Terrell, Raymond D. & Lindsey, Randall B. "Culturally proficient leadership: Doing what's right for students—all students." In Portelli, John P., & Griffiths, Darrin, eds. *Key Questions for Educational Leaders* (Burlington, ON: Word & Deeds Publ. Inc, 2015).

- The first cycle, Intention, exemplifies the real-world juxtaposition of *Barriers vs. Guiding Principles*. This first cycle is important because *it demonstrates competing underlying core values of deficit-based versus asset-based values and approaches.*
- The second cycle, Assessment, presents the *Continuum*'s broad reach from destructive behavior and policies (i.e., Cultural Destructiveness, Incapacity, and Blindness) to constructive behavior and policies (i.e., Cultural Precompetence, Competence, and Proficiency). It is here that the *Guiding Principles* serve as asset-based core values to inform individual and institutional values and actions that come to life in Cultural Precompetence, Competence, and Proficiency. Moreover, educators and schools that function in this part of the Continuum respond constructively to the negative values and behaviors given to the left side of the Continuum (i.e., Destructiveness, Incapacity, and Blindness).
- The third cycle, Action, intentionally identifies personal and institutional barriers to access and equity, embraces the guiding principles, and employs the Essential Elements as standards for assessing and planning behaviors, strategies, policies, and practices (Terrell & Lindsey, 2015).

GOING DEEPER

This chapter built on the introduction of the Tools of Cultural Proficiency in chapter 2 to present the tools in alignment with four key school functions, to describe how learning about the cultures of our migrant families and communities is an important professional learning activity, and to discuss the important role that we all play as leaders in service of our varied professional roles. Now is the opportunity to return to your journal and to individually reflect on the material in this chapter and/or to engage colleagues dialogically about your practice.

Reflective Activity

In what ways has this chapter informed your thinking about your professional learning and your role as a leader? What are some goals you might not want to set for yourself as a learner and as a leader? Please use your journal to record your comments.

Dialogic Activity

Keeping in mind that dialogue is for the purpose of participants' understanding of one another in ways you can move toward proving improved opportunities for children and youth from migrant families and communities, how might your learning community respond to the following prompt: *In what ways does this chapter inform your thinking about how you, as a learning community, embrace the opportunity to learn about migrant families and their communities? How might you proceed in the coming months?*

Think deeply about the prompts and, when ready, engage in in-depth discussion with colleagues for the purpose of exploring one another's thinking in a nonjudgmental manner. Remember, this activity is not for making decisions or plans, but only to explore one another's thinking.

Chapter 4 continues the journey of understanding culturally proficient actions through the use of a field-tested rubric. The chapter serves as a guide for you and your colleagues to be increasingly effective while working with all students, in particular with children and youth from migrant families and communities.

Chapter 4

Educators' Rubric for Inclusion and Support of Migrant Education Students, Their Families, and Their Communities

Moving beyond Rhetoric

Many rubrics describe a progression of skill from novice to expert. Our quest is, not for a rubric of skill development but for a rubric that combines insight and performance related to understanding of ideas and meaning.

—Wiggins and McTighe

GETTING CENTERED

Take a few moments to reflect on the comments you would have heard made by colleagues, community members, or the general public about children of migrant farmworkers, migrant students, programs that support their educational needs, or parents or guardians of your migrant students. Listen, reflect, and mentally paint a picture as to what your colleagues are saying. What assumptions do you hear being made about the migrant students? Migrant families? Migrant families' lifestyles?

OPPORTUNITY TO JOURNAL

In your journal, record the key words you are hearing and then take some time to mentally uncover the assumptions implied in those words.

In chapter 1, you were introduced to the importance of educating migrant children as well as their families, including out-of-school youth and the many types of migrant education programs and services that are available to migrant families. Yet, we know that educational and social services challenges still exist that historically have benefited by having migrant families and students live in those communities.

Our ethical role for teaching and working with migrant students and their families does not end at the doorsteps of our schools and classrooms. Schools are charged with teaching all students, yet immigrant and migrant students and their families are the least effectively served due to their educational levels, socioeconomic status, English-language proficiency, and, in many cases, unauthorized immigrant status.

"Teaching English to these students has often been roiled in issues of nativism, anti-immigrant fervor, and resistance to learning curricular and instructional strategies appropriate to English learning students" (Quezada, Lindsey & Lindsey, 2012, p. 36). This scenario includes migrant students, many of whom are English-learning students. Therefore, as a nation we have an ethical obligation and an opportunity to demonstrate how we value migratory families' linguistic and cultural assets, their funds of knowledge, as well as our schools' ability to provide our migrant students with the knowledge and skills needed to be successful in a multilingual, multicultural, global society.

Chapter 2 engaged us about the importance of our personal and professional learning to reflect on and about our practice along with the manner in which dialogue supports our examining school-based policies and prevalent practices. In this chapter, we introduce you to the Educators' Rubric for Inclusion and Support of Migrant Education Students, their Families, and their Communities to bring together three important factors: topics about instructing migrant students and supporting their families, reflection on our practices, and opportunities for individual or group dialogue as professionals. After the rubric, we delve more deeply and present a structured model of reflection for your consideration and use.

This chapter brings together for you, the reader, an opportunity to be meaningfully invested in your own professional learning. You are now familiar with the Five Essential Elements of Cultural Competence and Proficiency (i.e., assessing cultural knowledge, valuing diversity, managing the dynamics of difference, adapting to diversity, and institutionalizing cultural knowledge) as topics of inquiry. These can be key questions (i.e., that begin with what, how, and why) for the purpose of inquiring deeply as to the extent to which the Four Key Functions of schools (i.e., curriculum and instruction, assessment, parents and community, and professional development and learning) serve to inhibit or facilitate student access to equitable educational opportunities and outcomes.

The rubric in this chapter is intended as an inquiry guide for you and for your school's and district's professional learning in assessing how well each demographic group of students is being served. Chapters 5–9 guide deeper considerations in providing ever-deeper descriptions of each row of the rubric (i.e., essential element) combined with vignettes as you engage in personal reflection coupled with colleague dialogues about individual and institutional applications of the essential elements.

MAKING MEANING OF THE RUBRIC

Table 4.1 presents the Educators' Rubric for Inclusion and Support of Migrant Education Students, Their Families, and Their Communities. The first column depicts the Essential Elements' operational descriptions of the role educators and their schools play in educating migrant students and their families. The actions are used as leverage points for personal, professional, school, and district improvement of the educational services provided to migrant students and their families.

The following guide is suggested for reading and interpreting Table 4.1:

- The rubric comprises rows and columns, with each row being highlighted successively in chapters 5–9. Each of the rows is one of the five standards, also referred to as an *Essential Element of Cultural Competence.*
- There are seven columns. Column 1, titled "Essential Elements," provides an operational definition of each Essential Element. The Essential Elements serve as leverage points of growth to be used by educators working with migrant students, families, and communities, as well as by school leaders for their personal, professional growth and with their schools' and districts' policy considerations.
- Columns 2 through 7 are the phases of the Cultural Proficiency Continuum.
- As you read from Cultural Destructiveness to Cultural Proficiency for each of the five Essential Elements, you are viewing these elements as specific points of action in the progression of change for educators and their schools and districts.
- Column 6 is titled *Cultural Competence.* Each of the descriptors in this column describes one of the Essential Elements of Cultural Competence. The language is in active voice and describes actions that can be taken today in schools. It is at Cultural Competence in the Continuum where behaviors and related actions are deemed to be "at standard."
- Column 7 is titled *Cultural Proficiency.* The description is intended to be future focused and enduring.

Table 4.1 Educators' Rubric for Inclusion and Support of Migrant Education Students, Their Families, and Their Communities

Essential Elements for Including and Supporting Migrant Students and Their Families	Informed by Barriers to Cultural Proficiency		
	Cultural Destructiveness	*Cultural Incapacity*	*Cultural Blindness*
Assessing Cultural Knowledge—Extent to which educators commit to learn about their own and others' culture(s). They use this information as assets for planning and implementing effective and socially just practices that assist and advantage migrant students in before-, after-school, summer and Saturday schools, and in the linguistically and culturally diverse communities they live.	Degrade linguistically and culturally the diversity of migrant students, their families, and their communities. A deficit approach is taken toward an immigrant's home country, and U.S. culture is valued over other cultures by educators. Suppress any allusion to students' home culture and language by executing policies, programs, and practices, thereby becoming barriers to your own empowerment and the empowerment of others.	Renounce any positive influence of students' migrant background, home language, and culture on students and use programs and practices to push forward language and cultural assimilation. Regard migrant students' background, home life, language, and cultural diversity of migrant families and communities as an impairment to student learning.	Reject or be inept in examining the school's acceptance of migrant families' language and culture and/or communities as assets to student achievement and empowerment. Contribute to or endorse a standardized method of continuous improvement for all students; however, use standardized and English-language only tests as the only means of measuring achievement regardless of migrant students' language and culture.
Valuing Diversity—Extent to which educators value the linguistically and culturally diverse migrant students and their community. Migrant students and their families are inclusive of people and cultures with viewpoints and experiences different from educators for the benefit of the school and the community.	Confess that the purpose of school is to assimilate migrant students into English-only speakers. They employ no accommodation for linguistically and culturally diverse migrant students, their cultures, their families, or their communities. Refuse to provide access to core curriculum, Family Biliteracy and School Readiness Program instructional materials with academic rigor, supplemental instructional curriculum, and related educational and health resources to support linguistically and culturally diverse migrant students.	Ignore diverse perspectives and experiences for purpose of promoting an assimilationist function of school. Educators oppose mandated Family Biliteracy and School Readiness Program language development requirements and openly regard supplemental programs as an unnecessary intrusion into the school day curriculum. Such interventions negatively impact overall school academic achievement.	Migrant students are assigned into classes, as are other students, with no consideration for their academic credit needs due to their mobility, as well as their language ability or fluency. Conform to district, state, or national minimal educational requirements for home, school, and family engagement, and make no further efforts to engage linguistically and culturally diverse migrant families and communities.

| Managing the Dynamics of Difference—Extent to which educators use problem-solving and conflict resolution strategies as ways to be inclusive of multiple perspectives and to teach others about the dynamics of cultures in contact with one another. | Suppress diverse thoughts and opinions about the educational needs of linguistically and culturally diverse migrant students, thereby refuse, oppose, or evade developing and proposing instructional curricular programs and best practices to meet migrant students' unique educational needs due to their families' migrant working mobility factors.
Call for migrant students and their families to obey and abide culturally unresponsive decision-making, problem-solving, and conflict resolution method and structure of the school district, region and/or county that maintains the status quo that marginalizes or silences migrant communities served. | Comply with stated or implied approaches to conflict that maintain the status quo, exclude or trivializes diverse perspectives of migrant families, and perpetuate a *one-size-fits-all* approach to educating a full range of migrant students.
Involves self with migrant education issues only to satisfy local, state, and federal compliance requirements. | Finds ways to avoid conflict and in doing so make minimal effort to solicit diverse points of view.
Analyze, identify, and inappropriately placed linguistically and culturally diverse migrant students by not using proper academic Family Biliteracy and School Readiness Program evidence or other appropriate assessments. |
| Adapting to Diversity—Extent to which cultural knowledge is embedded into a moral understanding that leads educator values and school policies to achieve equitable educational and socially just outcomes. | Determines that the multilingualism and diverse culture migrant students and families bring to school, as well as their culture, disrupt their educational process.
Refuses pluralism as being part of curricula and best practices and believes the traditional school values enacted by the schools or districts are in the best interest of all migrant students. | Provides opportunities for migrant students and their families to take advantage of existing school programs and opportunities, provided to all students while making no linguistic or cultural accommodations for the migrant students, and then blame families or guardians as lacking interest in their students' academic success when they do not participate. | Ignore the belief that school, district, region, county, and the state have an important role in closing cultural and achievement gaps, which leads to explaining academic disparities in terms of external factors such as language learning, social class, student mobility, perceptions of parental education, or ethnicity and race. |

(Continued)

Table 4.1   Educators' Rubric for Inclusion and Support of Migrant Education Students, Their Families, and Their Communities

Essential Elements for Including and Supporting Migrant Students and Their Families	Informed by Barriers to Cultural Proficiency		
	Cultural Destructiveness	Cultural Incapacity	Cultural Blindness
Institutionalizing Cultural Knowledge—Extent to which cultural knowledge is evident in educator conduct and in school socially just policies and practices that address educational inequities and tend to close cultural and academic access, opportunity, and achievement gaps. Advocates for equitable and socially just policies and practices in the use of data to inform school of all migrant student and family needs.	Evade using academic and Family Biliteracy and School Readiness Programs or related achievement data to understand the school's effectiveness with linguistically and culturally diverse migrant students or to apprise of conversations, and decisions are guided by predominant assumptions and biases about migrant students that are unchallenged. Forgo or resist any and all responsibility for exploring institutional obstacles to teaching and learning about linguistically and culturally diverse migrant students. Relegate or exclude migrant Family Biliteracy and School Readiness Programs from the core curriculum by sustaining the credence that some linguistically and culturally diverse migrant students are not ready or capable of reaching higher forms of academic achievement.	Use academic Family Biliteracy and School Readiness Program achievement data to develop learning interventions and remediation programs that limit student access to content standards and core curriculum and, therefore, deny access to higher levels of academic achievement. Criticize migrant students' and their parents' or guardians' cultures and languages, other than standard forms of English, as foremost impediments to their success in school and society. Endorse the primary role of the school to remediate the linguistic and cultural "deficiencies" in language development that limit student Family Biliteracy and School Readiness Program success in school.	Use academic and Family Biliteracy and School Readiness Program achievement data with the purpose of improving the appearance of the school and without attention to the curricular and instructional needs of linguistically and culturally diverse migrant students. Consent narrow policies and practices that fail to benefit all students equitably. Fail to believe that the persistence of achievement gaps in Family Biliteracy and School Readiness Programs is tied to schools' failure to embrace migrant students' cultures and language. Plan for minimal Family Biliteracy and/or School Readiness Program achievement targets that are compliance-based and do not consider persistent access and achievement disparities.

Table 4.1 Educators' Rubric for Inclusion and Support of Migrant Education Students, Their Families, and Their Communities

Essential Elements for Including and Supporting Migrant Students and Their Families	Informed by Guiding Principles of Cultural Proficiency		
	Cultural Precompetence	Cultural Competence At Standard	Cultural Proficiency
Assessing Cultural Knowledge— Extent to which educators commit to learn about their own and others' culture(s). They use this information as assets for planning and implementing effective and socially just practices that assist and advantage migrant students in before-after-school, summer and Saturday schools, and in the linguistically and culturally diverse communities they live.	Recognize gaps in one's and colleagues' information about migrant students, families, and community cultures as assets. Assure to you and your school's ongoing learning about culturally and language diverse migrant students, their families and communities, or jeopardize regression to Cultural Blindness or unhealthier practices in the continuum.	Study and validate knowledge about the diverse cultures and languages of migrant families, and their community you work with in genuine ways through culturally relevant and socially just instruction and inclusion of the migrant lifestyle in core curricula. Employ the objectives identified by local and state Comprehensive Migrant Education Program Needs Assessments and the State Service Delivery Plan (SSDP) as well as school and community resources to access educational and College to Career Readiness opportunities for migrant students' success. Consider the linguistically and culturally diverse migrant family and community as an asset. Recognize how other educators and the school as a whole respond to the linguistically and culturally diverse migrant families and community you serve; and endlessly learn how to be active and effective in serving the migrant community. Examine and critique your linguistically and culturally diverse school and its grade levels and departments as cultural entities.	Teach using Individual Learning Plans (ILPs) as benchmark to address sociocultural inequities in the achievement of your linguistically and culturally diverse migrant students. Campaign for Out of School Youth and Priority for Service Migrant Students' (PfS) linguistic and culturally diverse academic and social success. Engage with school, district, and migrant families' Parent Advisory Councils (PACs) and community agencies and other resources in a collaborative method that engages them as partners in the education of all students through strong Regional Applications (RA) and/ or District Service Agreements (DSA). Utilize and develop partnerships with the Binational Migrant Teacher Exchange program as a venue to support school districts' knowledge about migrant students' and their families' cultural assets from their home countries.

(Continued)

Table 4.1   Educators' Rubric for Inclusion and Support of Migrant Education Students, Their Families, and Their Communities

Essential Elements for Including and Supporting Migrant Students and Their Families	Informed by Guiding Principles of Cultural Proficiency			
	Cultural Precompetence	Cultural Competence At Standard	Cultural Proficiency	
Valuing Diversity—Extent to which educators value the linguistically and culturally diverse migrant students and their community. Migrant students and their families are inclusive of people and cultures with viewpoints and experiences different from educators for the benefit of the school and the community.	Educators acknowledge having limited knowledge about educational barriers of linguistically and culturally diverse migrant students due to their families' mobility, their families' culture, and their communities. Educator is committed to expanding the District Service Agreements (DSA or Regional Applications (RA or both by learning about the diverse culture of migrant families and communities it serves. Educator states willingness to learn about Family Biliteracy and School Readiness Programs, techniques and strategies that better serve linguistically and culturally diverse migrant students. Educator supports techniques which foster an understanding and trust among migrant students and their families. Educator employs instructional strategies that may be inconsistently applied among linguistically and culturally diverse migrant students due to their unique agricultural mobility.	Offer district (PAC), Region (RAC), and State (SPAC) Parent Advisory Councils leadership opportunities by modeling and promoting culturally responsive techniques to meet the educational needs of your linguistically and culturally diverse migrant student community. Linguistically and culturally diverse migrant families and their communities are central to conversations, decision making, and problem solving by the school, school district, and its community. Educators are part of these processes including an engagement with the same content standards and core curriculum and engagement that results in higher academic achievement for migrant students. Lead and assist in Parent Advisory Councils and migrant parent conferences and meetings using linguistically and culturally appropriate communication or translations for verbal and written communication.	Using ILPs as benchmark, advance and develop mechanisms for creating a socially just school and society with particular emphasis on College to Career Readiness for Out-of-School Youth and Priority for Service Migrant Students who are linguistically and culturally diverse. Constantly engage in all aspects of your school community to collaborate on common goals and share educational and community resources. Engage in enhancing access of opportunity and eliminating achievement gaps, with particular attention paid to Out-of-School Youth and Priority for Service Migrant Students who are linguistically and culturally diverse.	

Managing the Dynamics of Difference—Extent to which educators use problem-solving and conflict resolution strategies as ways to be inclusive of multiple perspectives and to teach others about the dynamics of cultures in contact with one another.

Participate in developing Family Biliteracy/School Readiness Programs as part of the Regional Applications (RA) or District Service Agreements (DSA) and skills in problem-solving and conflict resolution strategies that are culturally responsive to migrant groups.

Gather and evaluate Family Biliteracy/School Readiness Programs as part of the Regional Applications (RA) or District Service Agreements (DSA), and academic assessments, as well as placement information on some migrant students that may be unreliable and/or inconsistent.

Weigh the associated benefits and risks to migrant students by examining programs such as Family Biliteracy/School Readiness Programs as part of the Regional Applications (RA) or District Service Agreements (DSA) of action.

Encourage and lead conversations that emerge into diverse opinions and perspectives across cultures and viewpoints as a usual and ordinary process within your school and the linguistically and culturally diverse migrant community it serves.

When facilitating conversations, anticipate and challenge resistance; then, take measures that may not be well liked but are deemed necessary in addressing the needs of a full range of migrant students within the linguistically and culturally diverse migrant communities your school serves.

Using ILPs as benchmark, resolve matters that arise among migrant cultural groups and families to fully understand about the school and community educational, and societal injustices experienced by Out-of-School Youth and Priority for Service Migrant Students who are linguistically and culturally diverse.

Work with Parent Advisory Councils and linguistically and culturally diverse migrant communities served by the school in a vigorous way to decipher and solve issues that are prevalent with Out-of-School Youth and Priority for Service Migrant Students and migrant communities served.

Adapting to Diversity—Extent to which cultural knowledge is embedded into a moral understanding that leads educator values and school policies to achieve equitable educational and socially just outcomes.

Nurture an authentic personal and school-wide sense of responsibility for learning about each and every migrant culture and language(s) spoken by the migrant community.

Study and learn about Regional Applications, District Service Agreements, and Comprehensive Needs Assessments.

Function as teams to effectively use Regional Applications, District Service Agreements, and Comprehensive Needs Assessments and Family Biliteracy and School Readiness Programs as well as achievement and access and opportunity data and culturally relevant instructional and curricular content standards to facilitate classroom discussions that represent the cultural and linguistic diversity of migrant students in an inclusive democratic environment.

Using Individual Learning Plans (ILPs) as benchmarks. Systematize school, district, and migrant Parent Advisory Councils and parent/guardian groups to examine, analyze and understand opportunity and access and academic achievement data in a way that considers divergent and often conflicting points of view and leads to equitable and just policies and practices.

(Continued)

Table 4.1 Educators' Rubric for Inclusion and Support of Migrant Education Students, Their Families, and Their Communities

Essential Elements for Including and Supporting Migrant Students and Their Families	Informed by Guiding Principles of Cultural Proficiency		
	Cultural Precompetence	Cultural Competence At Standard	Cultural Proficiency
	Demonstrate knowledge in order to disaggregate the academic achievement data and to work with colleagues to interpret and plan for effective use of the data in ways that ensure student academic and personal and social success for all linguistically and culturally diverse migrant students. Build on an initial awareness on the positive reasons of having Regional Applications, District Service Agreements, and Comprehensive Needs Assessments and Family Biliteracy and School Readiness Programs on the importance of disaggregating, analyzing and examining access and opportunity data that explores for disparities among linguistically and culturally diverse migrant students in special education, advanced placement classes, extracurricular activities, and student discipline.	Expound migrant students' ability to access College to Career Readiness and knowledge, and to meet the same challenging academic content standards, make decisions, solve problems, and develop dispositions that will benefit them in an interactive intercultural society.	Confront restrictive legal mandates and catalyze effective efforts intended to meet the needs of all students, with particular attention to Out-of-School Youth and Priority for Service Migrant Students who are linguistically and culturally diverse.
Institutionalizing Cultural Knowledge—Extent to which cultural knowledge is evident in educator conduct and in school socially just policies and practices that address educational inequities and tend to close cultural and academic access, opportunity, and achievement gaps.	Recognize through data analyses that Family Biliteracy and School Readiness Program achievement gaps are persistent and begin to pay attention to inequities inherent in student access and opportunity that leads to inappropriate academic placement.	Promote and support Regional Applications, District Service Agreements, and Comprehensive Needs Assessments and Family Biliteracy and School Readiness Programs in order to sponsor opportunities for sharing expertise among school personnel to address access and College and	Using ILPs as benchmarks, advocate for socially just and equitable policies and practices derived from the use of College to Career Readiness and academic data to inform school of migrant student needs, with particular emphasis on Out-of-School Youth and Priority for Service Migrant Students who are linguistically and culturally diverse.

Advocates for equitable and socially just policies and practices in the use of data to inform school of all migrant student and family needs.	Start to question the unequal distribution of available and appropriate human, educational, health, and financial resources that support professional development for appropriately serving linguistically and culturally diverse migrant students. Risk being overwhelmed by the size of closing academic achievement gaps for migrant students and decide to do little or nothing, and revert to counterproductive practices and policies.	Career Readiness opportunities for linguistically and culturally diverse migrant students and families. Deliberately seek input from linguistically and culturally diverse communities, inclusive of those who do not assert their voices or perspectives, to address access and achievement issues for their children. Measure Regional Applications, District Service Agreements, and Comprehensive Needs Assessments and Family Biliteracy and School Readiness Programs to align policies and practices to make equitable decisions that consider all community members' input, with particular focus on linguistically and culturally diverse migrant students.	Pursue to use College to Career Readiness and academic data to inform school progress in narrowing and closing academic achievement gaps of Out-of-School Youth and Priority for Service Migrant Students who are linguistically and culturally diverse.
	Actively utilize the Migrant Student Information Network and Migrant Student Record Exchange system to inform the school district, county, region, and state on how to allow migrant students an opportunity to accrue loss of school credits due to their or their families' agricultural migrant mobility.	Apply an evidence-based Regional Applications, District Service Agreements, and Comprehensive Needs Assessments, and Family Biliteracy and School Readiness Programs to support College to Career Readiness educational programs and consistently follow student placement decisions established on multiple academic and cultural measures that include language proficiency (i.e., English and home).	Coach colleagues and community members to develop and use Regional Applications, District Service Agreements, and Comprehensive Needs Assessments, and Family Biliteracy and School Readiness Programs to inform them about culturally proficient communication strategies to facilitate an understanding among the larger community that meeting the needs of linguistically and culturally diverse migrant students contributes to and supports the education of all students.

(Continued)

Table 4.1 Educators' Rubric for Inclusion and Support of Migrant Education Students, Their Families, and Their Communities

Essential Elements for Including and Supporting Migrant Students and Their Families	Informed by Guiding Principles of Cultural Proficiency		
	Cultural Precompetence	Cultural Competence At Standard	Cultural Proficiency
		Ensure that all secondary migrant students reach challenging academic standards and graduate with a high school diploma (or complete a GED) that prepares them for responsible citizenship, further learning, and productive employment. Apply and seek funding for an array of innovative and additional Migrant Education Initiatives to support the academic achievement of elementary, secondary, and college migrant students (i.e., College Assistance Migrant program (CAMP), High School Equivalence Program (HEP), Migrant Mini-Corps), as well as Teacher, Regional, and State Student and Parents Leadership Programs and Institutes. Develop national leadership initiatives to increase the capacity of state educational agencies, local school districts, schools, and other community organizations to continuously improve the educational outcomes attained by migrant students.	Integrate the Innovative Educational Technologies system nationally in order to increase the academic achievement of migrant students. Provide support systems and academic opportunities so that all secondary migrant students meet the academic standards to graduate with a high school diploma (or complete a GED) that prepares them to be College and Career Ready to be admitted to an institution of higher education so they may be responsible and productive citizens, and increase their employment opportunities. Institutionalizes an array of migrant education programs to support elementary, secondary and college migrant students after funding (in some instances) has been depleted or is no longer available, such as College Assistance Migrant program (CAMP), High School Equivalence Program (HEP), and Migrant Mini-Corps.

Source: Adapted from Reyes L. Quezada, Delores B. Lindsey, & Randall B. (2012). Lindsey, *Cultural Proficiency Practice-Educators Supporting English Learning Students,* Thousand Oaks, CA: Corwin.

The Intentional Use of "Educator": It is an inclusive term for policymakers, administrators, teachers, and counselors.

MAKING MEANING OF THE RUBRIC ACTIVITY

Effective use of the rubric involves being able to guide self and others to recognize nuances of language and embedded assumptions and misconceptions. The two activities that follow will support and deepen your understanding of the rubric and the role of educators when using the Essential Elements as leverage points for change. The activities are also highly effective professional development activities for your reflective use or as dialogic activities with colleagues.

It is our experience that when engaged with analyzing the rubrics, educators can "see" with new eyes; so feel free and do not be afraid to highlight or write in your book for this particular activity.

Adjectives and Verbs Activity

This first activity is to help you analyze the rubric to better understand and be able to use the rubric as a needs assessment, diagnostic, and planning tool. We suggest these steps:

- Focus your attention to the first essential element, *Assessing Cultural Knowledge*.
- Review and learn the *operational definition* of Assessing Cultural Knowledge in the first column. We refer to this definition as the "essence" of the essential element.
- Next, *read the many examples* in each of the cells and columns for *Assessing Cultural Knowledge*, beginning with *Cultural Destructiveness* and through *Cultural Proficiency*. You will have read six illustrations along each of the Continuum points.
- Having read all six illustrations, go back through each cell and circle, underline, or highlight all of the *verbs* and *adjectives* you can find. What do you notice as you read from left to right? Record your observations and reactions on the rubric.
- If conducting the activity with colleagues, compare and discuss your observations and reactions.
- Finally, perform the same analysis with the remaining four essential elements—Valuing Diversity, Managing the Dynamics of Difference, Adapting to Diversity, and Institutionalizing Cultural Knowledge.

By engaging and completing this activity, you will be equipped to use the rubric to assess, diagnose, and formatively develop your values and behaviors and your school's policies and practices when teaching or working with migrant students and their families. In the section below, we provide dialogic considerations of the rubric to further engage you and your colleagues in examining and engaging in continuous improvement of your educational practice.

Reflection Activity

Please use your mindful thinking as well as your journal to record your observations and reactions to the "Adjectives and Verbs" activity. What did you observe? What are your reactions? In what ways does the activity inform your understanding of the Essential Elements as standards for teaching and working with migrant students and their families?

± Assumptions Activity

This next activity engages you in closer reviewing and analyzing the rubric by reading beneath the two vertical columns, *Informed by Barriers to Cultural Proficiency* and *Informed by the Guiding Principles of Cultural Proficiency*. Follow these steps to further guide your inquiry:

- Read the 15 cells headed by *Informed by Barriers to Cultural Proficiency* and note the assumptions, both negative and positive, embedded in the descriptions and illustrations.
- Summarize the assumptions for later reference.
- Now read the 15 cells headed by *Informed by the Guiding Principles of Cultural Proficiency* and note the assumptions embedded in the descriptions and illustrations.
- As with the previous step, summarize the assumptions.
- Examine the two sets of assumptions. In what ways do they seem similar and different? What are your observations and reactions to the assumptions you have uncovered?
- If conducting the activity with colleagues, compare and discuss your mental or written journal observations and reactions.

After having completed the *Verbs and Adjectives* and *assumptions* activities, you are now prepared to use the rubric in your own professional practice and with colleagues in service to your total student population, with particular emphasis on your migrant students, families, and program services.

Reflection

Return to your mindful thinking or your journal and note your observations and reactions to the assumptions activity. What did you see? What are your reactions? In what ways does the activity inform your understanding of the Essential Elements as standards for teaching and working with migrant students and their families?

CYCLES OF REFLECTION

To this point in the book we have made abundant reference to reflection, and it is appropriate to take a few moments and share with you a model of reflection that we find useful. If experienced with practiced reflection, this section may be a useful review. We begin with Atkins and Murphy's Cycle of Reflection (1994), which pairs well with the developmental nature of the Tools of Cultural Proficiency.

Turn your attention to Figure 4.1. Begin at the top with Action of New Experience and follow the arrows through the six points of the cycle. We consider these points to be decision points because you can now be mindful about your own thinking. Put another way, you are thinking about your own thinking. You have the opportunity to take in new information and either affirm or change your thinking and the assumptions that inform your thinking.

Now take a moment to think back (i.e., reflect) on the first two activities in this chapter—Verbs and Adjectives along with Assumptions. Let's now bring that learning forward and apply it to the Cycle of Reflection. As you move along this cycle, you may become aware of uncomfortable feelings when considering the negative assumptions knowingly or unknowingly held by you, as well as the negative assumptions expressed by your colleagues.

You may recall from Figure 2.1 that this feeling of being uncomfortable is referred to as the *Zone of Ethical Tension*. As we examine and identify assumptions based in negative thinking, we move productively along the Continuum to uncover blind spots and move to initial awareness that is fundamental to effectiveness with students from migrant families.

This heightened awareness of viewing others' cultures as assets and being receptive to learning is Cultural Precompetence. This point of receptivity provides an educator or a group of educators entrée to using the Five Essential Elements of Cultural Competence and Proficiency as standards to guide educators' professional learning and their schools' consideration of policies and practices that intentionally embrace migratory families and their students.

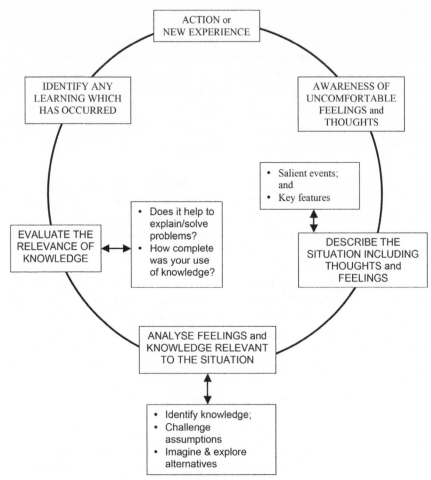

Figure 4.1   Atkins and Murphy's Cycle of Reflection. *Source*: Atkins S., & Murphy K. (1994) "Reflective Practice." *Nursing Standard* 8(39): 49–5.

GOING DEEPER

Personal and Professional Reflection: In reviewing your thoughts about the rubric and the two activities, *Adjectives and Verbs* and *assumptions/misconceptions*, what are you beginning to learn or affirm about your views regarding migrant students and their families? What new insights, if any, are you seeing about instruction, program policies, and practices?

Please continue further journaling or mindful thinking in order to better understand the Educators' Rubric for Inclusion and Support of Migrant Education Students, Their Families, and Their Communities.

Dialogic Activity

Now that you have reviewed, analyzed, and engaged yourself in the rubric and the two related activities, what do you view as the strengths of your current policies and practices and approaches to teaching and working with migrant students and their families? Where along the rubric would you locate your current policies and practices and approaches? What might be the underlying assumptions of those policies and practices and approaches? What might be the changes you would make to your curriculum or instructional approaches or both as well as policies and practices in order to better serve migrant students and their families? What do you, your colleagues, and your school, district, or migrant personnel need to learn and how might that learning inform your professional development plans for the next year or two?

YOUR ROLE IN SUPPORTING MIGRANT STUDENTS AND THEIR FAMILIES

Chapters 1–4 have provided you the introduction to using this book as a guide to examine and, if needed, reevaluate your values, beliefs, and practices about serving migrant students and their families. Chapters 5 through 9 will use the Essential Elements of Cultural Proficiency to guide you and your colleagues further on the learning journey in developing culturally proficient educational practices and policies. You will meet members of the Esperanza County and community.

These vignettes represent migrant education programs, whose regions include schools and districts that serve migrant students and their families and in which the authors have consulted for many years. These chapters also include a variety of professional resources and ideas to further support your and your colleagues' journey toward being able to even better assist migrant students and their families in your local district, regional, state, and national migrant programs.

Part II

ESSENTIAL ELEMENTS

ESPERANZA COUNTY AND PRÓXIMA ESTACIÓN SCHOOL DISTRICT: A FRAMEWORK FOR BUILDING CULTURAL PROFICIENCY WITHIN MIGRANT EDUCATION PROGRAMS

Through the next few chapters (5–9) we ask that you challenge yourself to engage in deeper learning by understanding and applying the Essential Elements of Cultural Proficiency. Chapters 5 through 9 each describe one Essential Element by defining and discussing the Essential Element as a standard for educator behavior when working with migrant students and their families, and in the development of effective socially just school policies and practices through each of the points in the cultural proficiency continuum.

A linear approach is not suggested as a one-for-one use of an Essential Element, but rather an approach that looks at the Essential Elements in a holistic manner as found in the rubric in chapter 4. We present the Essential Elements in each of the chapters to facilitate a deeper understanding and mastery of each of the elements in the rubric.

The Essential Elements are brought together in chapter 10 as the final product that will result in a 2-day professional learning staff development training tailored to the needs of the reader and her or his county office, school, or district. The staff development will be framed in a manner that is cohesive for individual and groups of educators, as well as for migrant education personnel to plan and develop more effective migrant education program services to successfully educate and assist migrant students and their families. Chapter 10 will take a proactive approach so that you and your colleagues may use the new language of Cultural Proficiency to assess where individuals are in the continuum.

Esperanza County

You will be introduced to assistant superintendents, teachers, coordinators, migrant education regional directors, recruiters, and parents who personified our experiences when working with migrant education programs. Throughout the chapters, you will be exposed to different scenarios representing various challenges faced by personnel aiming to evaluate, enhance, and apply new practices when working with Priority for Services *(PFS)* students.

The Board of Education of Esperanza County has identified a goal for the upcoming fiscal year to develop effective programs that meet the wide range of needs of all PF students. In response to the board's initiative "Best Practices, a Priority for All," the assistant superintendent has put together a leadership team that will identify programs designed for cultural competent educators committed to overcome deficit approaches when working with PF students. The leadership team is working to ensure: (a) programs are tailored to the specific needs of PF students as well as aligned with the Comprehensive Needs Assessment (CNA) findings, and (b) educators working in the implementation of these programs are culturally competent to apply additive models that potentiate the skills, language, and knowledge PF students and their families bring to the learning processes.

Chapter 5

Assessing Cultural Knowledge— From Self-Centered Learning to Socially Just Student- and Community-Asset Learning

[There are educators] . . . who are so talented and committed that they manage to find ways to enable their students to achieve well beyond the expectations that others hold for them based on their race and class.

—Pedro Noguera (2008, p. 194)

GETTING CENTERED

Take a few moments to think about yourself as an educator—teacher, aide, counselor, administrator, or district support personnel. First, think about yourself in relation to your school (or district). Second, think about the migrant neighborhoods or communities served by your school or district.

If you are new to the education profession, this activity and chapter will support you in two ways. You will develop the ability to navigate effectively among and build a strong relationship with your new colleagues. Second, you will begin an extended journey of learning about the migrant community—in all its diversity—served by your school and to embrace the entire community as it grows or changes demographically.

This activity is designed to support you in learning more about yourself as a cultural being as well as to support you in learning more about the culture of your school or district and the community served by your school (or district).

OPPORTUNITY TO JOURNAL

Take a few moments and return to your journal to consider and respond to these questions:

- To what extent are you knowledgeable about your own culture and the effect your culture may have on the students and the community from which they come, with particular emphasis on students from migrant families?
- In what ways would you describe the academic culture of the school or district?
- How would you describe you and your colleagues' knowledge about the diversity of cultures in the community you serve?

As you take time to think about these questions, turn to your journal and record your response to the questions that resonate for you.

ASSESSING CULTURAL KNOWLEDGE

Learning about Migrant Students and Migrant Farmworker Communities through a Transformative and Socially Just Lens

There is a need to be transformative educators while working with migrant students and their families. Being transformative is to acknowledge and assess our own language and cultural knowledge as well as the transformative processes that will take place in your and your school's learning about the many communities served by your school or district. What we know and how much we know about our own cultural and language heritage is sometimes an indication about how much we are willing to learn about migrant students and their families, other communities and the communities they live in, as well as knowing about the cultural and language heritage of our own colleagues.

As we delve into the important work of meeting the needs of our students from migratory families, it is worth taking a few minutes to differentiate between three words—transactional, transformational, and transformative—as they are used in the field of education. These words are not inconsequential parsing of terms that may appear to be similar, but reflect deeply held values about the extent to which educators are knowledgeable about and involved with the communities they serve. Shields describes three types of leadership, each of which is necessary in today's demographically complex schools:

- *Transactional leadership* involves a mutual agreement where both parties benefit from the decisions made. For example, a decision as per which school members and parents agree to hold regularly scheduled meetings in which educators provide feedback about their children's progress is trans-actional leading.

• *Transformational leadership* focuses on improving organizational effec-tiveness. Continuing with the previous example of improving student prog-ress, parents and school members engage regularly scheduled sessions in which school members and parents learn skills and strategies that support students' literacy development.

• *Transformative leadership* recognizes that gaps in student literacy exist as well as educational inequities that are often generational and correlated with students' migratory status. School members and parents work together to challenge practices that render students incapable of higher order learn-ing and to commit themselves to equitable academic access and outcomes (Shields, 2010; Lindsey, Kearney, Estrada, Terrell, & Lindsey, 2015).

When school members—teachers, counselors, and administrators—interact with parents and community members, in particular those from migratory families, all educators are viewed and received as "leaders." Though we in the educational community hold fast on various distinctions about leadership, it is important to look into our organizational mirror and acknowledge that in addition to the formal leadership roles of principal and superintendent, among many others, we also are fully aware of the many colleagues who are recognized as nonformal leaders, for which there is no title.

When interacting with a group of parents and community members—in the context of this book, parents of students from migratory communities—we must be mindful that coming together to reduce the effects of identifiable inequities promotes a sharing of perspectives that can lead to mutual under-standings that promote socially just and equitable outcomes for students.

If we and our colleagues are knowledgeable of the needs, as well as the assets, traditions, and customs that our migrant students and their families bring, then true transformative change can begin to take place. Imagine that your school and the community have had an influx of migrant farm-worker families due to farmers changing their farming crops. The new crops planted will now require picking fruits and vegetables by hand for the next four months instead of the traditional planting cycle of alfalfa or wheat that only required machinery and one person to drive the tractor or hay bailer.

These new community members may include migrant farmworker families from the central and southern rural part of Mexico as well as from Central America. Many might also be from Mexican and Central American indig-enous groups such as Triqui, Mixteco, or Mayan, many of whom do not speak or speak little Spanish. Some might also be Somali Muslims, who have found it difficult to find employment in urban areas, whose language, culture, and dress is unique and different from the many students in your school.

Long-term residents of the community of which you are part of may believe that the language and faith of their community is superior to the migratory workers or that newly introduced traditions will clash with what the town and school have historically acknowledged and celebrated. Such attitudes give rise to the negative stereotyping of the new families as well as their children.

A transformative approach might be for the educators and community members to be willing to learn more about and from the new migrant farm-worker families and their children, even if it is for a short period of time due to farm-working families moving to a neighboring state as they continue to follow and pick seasonal crops.

AN INQUIRY ACTIVITY

Do you know the number of students served by your school (or district, if the school district is more relevant to your role)? If you are a site-based educator, do you know the students from migrant families? How would you begin to find answers to these questions? Turn to your journal to record your responses to these questions. Be as candid as possible. This is about your learning and increased effectiveness as an educator and only you will know your responses. Once you have completed this activity, continue into the next section. We will pick up the activity later in the chapter.

WHAT CAN WE DO AS EDUCATORS?

As educators what steps can you take to learn about the migrant farmworker families, their children and the cultural and language assets they will bring to the school and to the community? How can you assess your own language and cultural knowledge about the linguistic and cultural assets of a particular migrant ethnic group, such as those from indigenous backgrounds? How would you start to learn what you know or do not know about the migrant farmworker families and the assets the children bring to your school? How can you lead and grow from your own learning, as well as with and for your colleagues?

These questions are important as a way to guide your own self-reflection and promote dialogue among members of the school and the community at large through reflective practice. As Ladson-Billings (2001) asserts, educators have had an increase of demands placed on them—first, with No Child Left Behind legislation, as well as Race to the Top and now with Common Core. Educators now have less time to reflect by viewing it as a luxury instead of a necessity to improve instructional programs and practices (Shealy, McHatton, & Vixon Wilson, 2011). It is hoped the new 2015 Elementary and Secondary Education Act authorization, Every Student Succeeds Act, supports our role as reflective educators engaging in ongoing curricular, instructional, and assessment improvement.

Transformative learning can take many forms; it begins with one's self and it then extends to our peers and the wider community. Most importantly, transformative practices guide us to learn about the organizational and systemic culture at our grade level, department, school, and the school district and the manner in which the school culture relates to migrant students and their families. In other words, is the culture of our school (or district) inclusive or not? Does our school send welcoming messages or does it send messages that, intentionally or not, rebuff students from migrant communities?

Learning and knowing about the school's systemic culture will support you in leading the learning about your own classroom, your school, your school district level, as well as your school board and its policy making regarding migrant education. To understand the systemic nature of organizational cultures, let's consider one or more of the following scenarios:

• Suppose you are the regional county migrant education director or the district migrant education coordinator for your school district and you attended multiple school- and grade-level meetings. As the results of migrant students' grade-level or language proficiency placement scores are being discussed. What differences do you notice in the procedures being followed or used and the manner in which individuals interact with each other?

• If you are a middle or secondary school educator who has a high number of migrant students teaching content courses, how do you and your colleagues from the different content area disciplines interact with one another in support of your migrant students? How is the data analyzed and how is it used?

• To what extent do you take into consideration students' migratory history, their attendance of different schools, and the difficulties associated with learning a new language? To what extent are these topics part of your culture of learning?

Assessing cultural knowledge occurs only when educators begin to learn about other cultures' "familial capital" (Bejarano & Velarde, 2012, p. 27). This includes "community history, memory, cultural intuition; in essence the cultural knowledge that is nurtured in the family" (Delgado Bernal, 2001) which includes customs, traditions, and language assets that Delgado Bernal (2002) coins "pedagogies of the home" that offer "culturally specific ways of teaching and learning and embrace[s] ways of knowing that extend beyond the public realm of formal schooling" (p. 110).

Knowing and understanding the ways in which farmworker migrant families teach and learn is as important as learning about the school. Educators can learn about the "pedagogies of the home" which can occur in an informal or formal manner with a focus on the integration of the cultural, language, and family assets into the classroom and school core curriculum as part of the broader academic common core to support rigorous instructional models for migrant students so migrant students may achieve the academic and personal or social success due to them and all students in your school.

Our role as educators is to create an educational system that promotes equitable and socially just teaching practices in our classrooms and across our school, the school district, and our community. Sonia Nieto along with her colleague Patty Bode (2006) defines social justice as "both a philosophy and actions that embody treating all people with fairness, respect, dignity, and generosity" (p. 2). Therefore, our role as an educator is to facilitate our and our schools' professional learning by being an educator who leads, not follows.

Promoting and collaborating with your colleagues begins by learning about effective migrant education program models such as presented in chapter 1. These models are indispensable when planning effective instructional and educational socially just practices. The beauty of these models and practices is that they serve all students in a socially just and equitable manner.

These models and practices are not learned in a vacuum but are best learned through collaboration with others. They are to be shared with others in transformative processes that radiate through your school and district into the community. Freire (1986) argued that "educators must be willing to see teaching as a revolutionary process, to look critically at the world, school district policies, the schools and their classrooms in order to recognize their own social and political reality. By recognizing their own social and political reality they will have the tools to change the educational systems" (p. 159). Assessing one's cultural knowledge is the first step and an essential element in the cultural proficiency journey as we recognize our role as culturally proficient educators in the inside-out journey taken by educators to make our classrooms, schools, and community a safe learning place for our migrant families and their children who are enrolled in our schools.

CULTURALLY RELEVANT AND PROFICIENT PRACTICES IN SUPPORT OF MIGRANT STUDENTS AND THEIR FAMILIES

Due to migrant farmworker families search of seasonal work in our nation's farms and factories, there are effective educator practices to be considered. When working with migrant students and their families one needs to take into account socially and just practices in order to fully engage migrant families and, in particular, *Priority for Service* migrant youth, in their educational experiences in schools. Schools serving migrant families need:

- Educators knowledgeable about the migrant lifestyle as well as about how the constant displacement of students might impede the educators' own learning about migrant students' cultures and students' prior experiences;
- Educators who advocate for migrant families and embrace their migratory community as a familial capital asset through valuing the heritage and history of migrant children's families. It is important to know and utilize local, state, and national programs as well as all school resources available to migrant families to access and provide opportunities for success (see Resources section);
- Educators need to know how other educators, the school community, and the wider community reacts to migrant families, their children, and communities;
- Educators who continuously learn how to be effective in serving their multiple migrant farmworkers' diverse communities—both domestic and families from other countries who serve as migrant seasonal workers. These may include many linguistic and culturally diverse indigenous communities;
- Educators who lead their school and its grade levels and departments by modeling and promoting culturally relevant and responsive methods of instruction to meet the learning needs of the migrant students;
- Educators who have the highest of expectations and utilize cooperative groups in their classrooms and support their students through ascending learning transitions by providing safe learning spaces for migrant students (Banks, 1993; Gay, 2000; Ladson-Billings, 1995; Mathur, 2011; Nieto, 2013, 2004).

These practices and roles represent paradigmatic shifts educators' transformative learning based in acquiring deep knowledge of community needs derived through personal, face-to-face interactions with members of migrant communities.

Being knowledgeable about the communities we have in contrast to the communities we used to have or that we wish we had makes us fully capable of shifting

- *From* remedial programs that promote language and cultural assimilation of migrant students into the dominant culture in ways that disavows any positive influence of students' home languages and cultures.
- *To* using students' migrant culture and possible native language as assets on which to build and promote academic and social success.

Transformative thinking engages educators in learning and leading that values language and culture as assets that is further developed in chapter 6. In so doing, Migrant students' ways of learning and knowing are valued and, thereby, students are provided equitable access and opportunity for academic and social success.

MINDFULNESS IS BEING INTENTIONAL

The following three sections present a series of mindfulness questions. This approach as defined by Langer (1997) has three characteristics: *the continuous creation of new categories; openness to new information; and, an implicit awareness of more than one perspective* (p. 4). These questions are designed to facilitate your mindfulness about possibility and flexibility. Mindful thinking is a process by which meaning is given through context and outcomes. Use these questions to guide your inside-out thinking and learning process. As appropriate, return to your journal to record your thinking:

OPPORTUNITY TO JOURNAL: MY INSIDE-OUT LEARNING PROCESS

- Who am I in relation to the students I teach or serve? In particular, who am I in relation to migrant students?
- What am I learning about myself in relation to migrant students?
- What are some indicators of success that I know about the cultures of my migrant students and families?
- What are some indicators of success that I use about the language and cultural knowledge of my students as assets toward their academic achievement?

INQUIRY II: FACILITATING YOUR SCHOOL'S INSIDE-OUT LEARNING PROCESS ABOUT SCHOOL CULTURE

School culture is indisputable as water is to a fish. However, most of us are somewhat oblivious because "it just is" for us. However, when we have new people entering the system, they have to learn what we value. People who have experiences similar to ours often "fit in" with little effort. However, people (i.e., educators, parents, students) whose culture may be different from the dominant culture may have to learn our school's culture in more direct or deliberate ways. This inquiry into your school's culture is important because it is designed to make what is accepted to be implicit and to be examined explicitly and publicly by you and your colleagues so you can know "what you intend" is what is experienced by those new to your school or district.

Without looking at your school or district's handbook, what do you understand the school or district's mission, vision or core values to be? No peeking, this is an important step and only you will know your responses. Use these prompts to guide your thinking:

- Who do we say we are as a school or district?
- Are we who we say we are?
- In what ways might we assess and examine our current school culture?
- In what ways may our school culture support or inhibit migrant students and their families?

Use your journal to record your responses. Once you have completed this activity, continue to the next section.

INQUIRY III: FACILITATING MY SCHOOL'S INSIDE-OUT LEARNING PROCESS ABOUT THE COMMUNITIES IT SERVES

Once you have begun to consider the school's culture, you are well prepared to begin in-depth learning about the community served by your school or district, with particular emphasis on migrant communities. This inquiry is best conducted with colleagues. A good place to begin is in dialogic conversation where you consider the questions below. Sharing perceptions and perspectives provides a beginning point for your continued learning.

- Who and where are the communities we serve?
- What might be the outcomes of viewing our communities as our cultural partners?
- In what ways might we serve and partner with our communities to support migrant students, many of whom are English-Learning students?
- What would be some indicators of success that our migrant students would benefit from a cultural community partnership?

Sharing your views and listening to the views of others in ways that are open and candid opens the door to the professional learning that follows in this book. Remember, it is always appropriate and helpful as you progress through this book to return to the already completed journal entries and to update your thinking as appropriate.

The "inside-out" thinking in which you and your colleagues have engaged in these first five chapters prepares you to meaningfully delve into the Five Essential Elements as presented in this chapter and continuing through chapter 9. You will develop the skill to "hear" messages that regard students' cultures as liabilities and the skill to "hear and deliver" messages that hold students' cultures, with particular emphasis on migrant students' cultures, as assets on which the school can build educator and student learning experiences.

THE RUBRIC IN ACTION: ASSESSING CULTURAL KNOWLEDGE FOR INCLUSION AND SUPPORT OF MIGRANT EDUCATION STUDENTS, THEIR FAMILIES, AND THEIR COMMUNITIES

The Essential Element-Assessing Cultural Knowledge functions as an "inside-out" process for you, your colleagues and your school's learning about migrant students' cultures. Consider the following two steps as you read to understand this initial element from the rubric:

* Step One: refer to chapter 4, Table 4.1, "Educators' Rubric for Inclusion and Support of Migrant Education Students, their Families, and their Communities" Reading from left to right across the row of the rubric, Assessing Cultural Knowledge, then read the progression from Cultural Destructiveness to Cultural Proficiency.
* Step Two: turn your attention to Table 5.1 below and note that it presents the Assessing Cultural Knowledge row of the rubric from chapter 4. Three things to note:
  o Table 4.1 includes only the "positive" side of the rubric. However, in your role as an educator you will hear comments and become aware of practices represented on the left side of the continuum. The rubric is designed for the right side to provide choices when responding to comments or practices located on the left side—which is represented as Cultural Destructiveness, Incapacity, or Blindness.
  o It is important to develop an awareness that comments or practices that may come from you and not always from colleagues may well, in fact, be found on the left side of the rubric. As you become aware of comments or practices located at any point of the rubric, the illustrations on the right side of the rubric can be used as suggested comments or practices for you and your colleagues. Recognizing and acknowledging the placement of comments or practices on the rubric represents the "inside-out" process of change for you and your school.
  o The illustrations for Cultural Precompetence, Competence, and Proficiency in Table 5.1 express intentional use of adjectives and verbs and

Table 5.1 Essential Element: Assessing Cultural Knowledge for Inclusion and Support of Migrant Education Students, Their Families, and Their Communities

Essential Elements for Including and Supporting Migrant Students and Their Families	*Informed by Guiding Principles of Cultural Proficiency*		
	Cultural Precompetence	*Cultural Competence at Standard*	*Cultural Proficiency*
Assessing Cultural knowledge— Extent to which educators pledge to learn about their own and others' culture(s). They use this information as assets for planning and implementing effective and socially just practices that assist and advantage migrant students in before-after-school, summer and Saturday schools and in the linguistically and culturally diverse communities they live.	Recognize misunderstandings in one's and colleagues' information about migrant students, families and community cultures as assets. Assure your school's ongoing learning about culturally and language diverse migrant students, their families and communities, or jeopardize regression to Cultural Blindness or unhealthier practices in the continuum.	Study and validate knowledge about the diverse cultures and languages of migrant families, and their community you work with in genuine ways through culturally relevant and socially just instruction and inclusion of the migrant lifestyle in core curricula. Employs the objectives identified by local and state Comprehensive Migrant Education Program Needs Assessments and the State Service Delivery Plan (SSDP) as well as school and community resources to access educational and College to Career Readiness opportunities for migrant student's success. Consider the linguistically and culturally diverse migrant family and community as an asset.	Teach using Individual Learning Plans (ILPs). Use them as benchmarks to address sociocultural inequities in the achievements of your linguistically and culturally diverse migrant students. Campaign for Out-of-School Youth and Priority for Service Migrant Students' (PFS) linguistic and culturally diverse academic and social success. Engage with school, district, and migrant families Parent Advisory Councils (PACs) and community agencies and other resources in a collaborative method that engages them as partners in the education of all students through strong Regional Applications (RA) and/or District Service Agreements (DSA). Utilize and develop partnerships with the Binational Migrant Teacher Exchange program as a venue to support school districts knowledge about migrant students and families cultural assets from their home countries.

(Continued)

Table 5.1 Essential Element: Assessing Cultural Knowledge for Inclusion and Support of Migrant Education Students, Their Families, and Their Communities

Essential Elements for Including and Supporting Migrant Students and Their Families	Informed by Guiding Principles of Cultural Proficiency		
	Cultural Precompetence	Cultural Competence at Standard	Cultural Proficiency
		Recognize how other educators and the school as a whole respond to the linguistically and culturally diverse migrant families and community you serve; and endlessly learn how to be active and effective in serving the migrant community. Examine and critique your linguistically and culturally diverse school and its grade levels and departments as cultural entities. Offer district (PAC), Region (RAC) and State (SPAC) Parent Advisory Councils leadership opportunities by modeling and promoting culturally responsive techniques to meet the educational needs of your linguistically and culturally diverse migrant student community.	

Source: Adapted from Reyes L. Quezada, Delores B. Lindsey, & Randall B. Lindsey. (2012). *Cultural Proficiency Practice-Educators Supporting English Learning Students,* Thousand Oaks, CA: Corwin.

active voice. Creating personal and organizational change is an intentional "inside-out" process for educators and their schools.

Changes to you and your school will be met with resistance by those who maintain that the students and their parents or guardians are the ones who need to conform to prevalent school practices. You may want to revisit the discussion in chapter 3 about how the Guiding Principles of Cultural Proficiency provide the moral framework of Cultural Proficiency and informs the right side of the rubric. The vignette that follows (Dr. Ceballos) models the "inside-out" approach to change for the (Esperanza County and Estación School District). As you read the vignette, pay particular attention to evidence of progression along the rubric and how the moral framework is represented in educators' actions.

This chapter begins a series of vignettes to demonstrate educators' use of school- and district-based applications of the Tools of Cultural Proficiency to the educational needs of students from migrant families. Chapters 6 through 9 continue the vignettes in storyboard fashion. Opportunities are provided for you to use your journals to reflect on your own learning and to chronicle insights gained from dialogue with colleagues.

The county, school district, and characters are fictional; however, they are consistent with our experiences in working across the United States and Canada. No doubt you will find some voices that are familiar—they may even be your voices. Enjoy the journey and your learning along the way.

VIGNETTE: ESPERANZA COUNTY AND PRÓXIMA ESTACIÓN SCHOOL DISTRICT

Esperanza County's assistant superintendent is meeting with the Migrant Education Program team—migrant education regional director, education county services coordinator, school district migrant directors and coordinators, identification and recruitment coordinator, recruiters and teachers working in supplemental programs (after-school, Saturday-school, and summer school)—to address the need of developing programs that meet the needs of Priority for Service (PF) students.

The last Comprehensive Needs Assessment conducted by an external evaluator reported that programs implemented in the region failed to address the specific needs of PF students. The superintendent at Esperanza County has underlined the importance of ensuring PF students are equipped with effective tools; thus, they can successfully face the challenges—linguistic, social, and cultural—they encounter when navigating the pre-K–12 educational system.

Let's listen to the opening comments at the monthly Migrant Education Program review meeting:

Dr. Ceballos, Assistant Superintendent:

*Thanks for joining me here today to begin the analysis of our programs and services. I have asked Mr. Perez to head up the Educational Programs team for what we are calling the Identifying Best Practices Retreat. The Board and the Superintendent have identified the search of best and effective practices for PFS students as one of the main goals for this year. As you know, the outcomes of the last Comprehensive Needs Assessment reflected the need for rethinking, redesigning, and reviewing how we as county office are meeting the needs of PFS students and their families. **The Comprehensive Needs Assessment is an evaluation tool that allow us to identify the areas in which we have to rethink our practices.***

As your Assistant superintendent, I've been asked by the Board and the Superintendent to make this goal a priority item for us and the school districts and to prepare a plan of action.

So, here we are today, ready to move forward by involving county personnel, district administrators, teachers, and recruiters in planning our actions. Mr. Perez, the room is yours.

Mr. Perez, Migrant Education Regional Director:

Gracias, Dr. Ceballos. First, let me say, thank you for being so open with us and sharing the directive of the Board and the Superintendent.

As members of the Migrant Education Program, we, too, want to ensure PF students are participating in high quality, research-based programs, which meet their specific needs. We have known there was a need for improvement but due to other needs we have lacked on analyzing different and effective ways in which PF students and their families could actively participate and reach the outcomes established in our past programs.

This is an exciting opportunity to discuss the outcomes of the CNA and how we can use these to transform our Migrant Education Program.

Ms. Marti, County Migrant Education Program Coordinator:

As you know Mr. Perez, every year when writing our Regional Application (RA) and overseeing how school districts complete their District Service Agreements (DSA), we have discussed the need for identifying culturally and linguistically responsive practices specifically designed for PF students. We know we have to rethink the way we serve our PFs as they are the ones who might face the most challenges and struggling when being part of education compulsory settings. We are collecting longitudinal data of PF students but up to this point, we have not deeply analyzed the trends within these sets of data.

Mr. Tamarit, District Migrant Education Program Coordinator— Próxima Estación School District:

Ms. Marti, we share the same sentiment. We have collected data and attempted to align what the data is telling us when designing the individual learning plans (ILP) of each PF student. We truly believe that a comprehensive approach involving all of us in this endeavor will help in our search, analysis, and implementation of culturally and linguistically responsive practices.

Ms. Wells, Teacher—Brownfield School District:

Yeah, Mr. Tamarit, we as teachers always thought that there was a need to better understand what a PF student is and how we can modify, adapt, and differentiate our practices both when teaching in migrant programs and when teaching migrant students throughout the regular school year. We want to enhance our practices, but honestly, we do not know how.

Ms. Ponce, PAC and RAC representative— Harvest School District:

It is good to hear the Board of Education is thinking about finding programs that can support our students. How can we parents support this process?

Mr. Mayoral, I & R County Coordinator:

I am listening to what you all are saying and I am thinking the effort should start as soon as we recruit students and see and evaluate what their needs are in terms of adapting to a new environment and overcoming the lack of belonging.

Ms. Peralta, Recruiter—County:

I agree with you Mr. Mayoral, we must work together to have a better understanding of our PF students. We as recruiters could contextualize academic reports with the stories students and families shared with us.

OPPORTUNITY TO JOURNAL GUIDING QUESTIONS

Turn to your journal to record responses to the following questions.

- As you think about the conversation among the Migrant Education Program Team, what might be some assumptions or misconceptions regarding PF students that prevent educators from deeply analyzing, designing, and implementing programs that meet the needs of PF students?
- What might be some beliefs held by the superintendent and the board regarding PF students, their needs, and challenges?
- If you were the migrant education program director responsible for the development and implementation of best practices, what might you say following the assistant superintendent's initial comment?

Returning to the Vignette:

The meeting continues as all the members begin to analyze data on the programs in which *PFS* students participated during the last year. They are closely analyzing the objectives and assessment tools as these are aligned with the trends highlighted in the ILP for *PFS* students.

Dr. Castells, the PI on the Comprehensive Needs Assessment, and his assistant Matthew Faulkner are next on the agenda.

Dr. Castells—External Evaluator:

Thank you all for sharing your thoughts on such important topic. When collecting and analyzing data for the CNA, we observed that PF students were participating in programs that somehow met their specific needs. We could not identify an alignment between the needs depicted on their ILPs and how these helped coordinators and teachers to adapt, modify the implementation of these programs. It seemed that the programs were too broad and lacked clarity on how each PF student was meeting the goals indicated on their ILPs.

Ms. Gutierrez, Teacher—Próxima Estación School District:

Thanks for sharing with us the outcomes of the CNA. We agree that we need more specification on the objectives, outputs, and outcomes when working with PF students. But, please do not ignore the successes we have had with some of these students.

Ms. Garmendia, Recruiter—Próxima Estación School District:

Don't forget how the program is helping PF students and their families to overcome all the challenges they experience on a daily basis. Our success stories are valuable.

Matthew Faulkner—Comprehensive Needs Assessment:

We witnessed these success stories. We just want to share what we observed, so that you can ensure all PF students participate in programs that meet their needs on the following areas:

- *Meet the benchmark set on district and state standardized assessments*
- *Have the support to overcome the lack of belonging and anonymization*
- *Have a well-designed ILP that can be implemented when (if) they move to another state.*

OPPORTUNITY TO JOURNAL

Use this opportunity with your journal to reflect on the vignette (either alone or with colleagues) and think deeply about what you just read. Consider the following questions:

- Why do you think Ms. Gutierrez and Ms. Garmendia insist on highlighting the success stories?
- Why is Dr. Castell emphasizing the idea of "meeting the specific needs of PFs"?
- How do you adapt your instruction (in your classroom) to meet the needs of PF students?
- Do you have access to ILPs? Has your school scheduled meetings to discuss the specific needs of PFs?

PLANNING AND PROVIDING FOR PROFESSIONAL LEARNING WITH A SOCIALLY JUST FOCUS FOR EDUCATORS WHO TEACH MIGRANT STUDENTS

We know that U.S. teachers are primarily white and many new credentialed teachers are assigned to schools that are part of communities with low socio-economic status and where the majority of the students are students of color, many of whom are English learners and, in rural areas, migrant students.

Therefore, effective professional learning development is key to the success of both teachers and students, including migrant students (Nieto, 2013; California Department of Education, 2010). Further, even though having a highly qualified teacher in every classroom is critical for every student, teachers themselves have reported that they lack the necessary knowledge and skills and often feel unprepared when working with migrant students, most of whom are also English learning students.

Nieto (2006) holds that social justice in education means reforming not only school policies but also instructional practices. She asserts that four components should be considered. The four components can easily be adaptable as a professional development tool in the planning of staff development and adapted for those educators working with migrant students. Nieto's Four Components support the Cultural Proficiency Essential Elements discussed in chapters 5–9:

- Educators should integrate themes and topics of inequality in the curriculum. This will ensure that migrant students—as they are often now—are not left out and are part of the conversation. This also forces courageous conversations as it "challenges, confronts, and disrupts misconceptions, untruths, and stereotypes that lead to structural inequality and discrimination based on race, social class, gender, and other social and humane differences" (p. 2). As a result of migrant students' mobility, language barriers, and low social economic status, migrant families cannot afford many educational resources.
- Authentic educational resources should be provided so that migrant students can optimize their potential. Books and literature in the curricula should have materials that represent their experiences–this will enhance their emotional well-being. Believing in migrant students' capabilities by holding the same high expectations for them and yet being able to adapt the teaching and curriculum is a must.
- It is important—this has been discussed throughout this book and it supports social justice—to acknowledge the strengths and assets that migrant families bring to their education and to the schools. Strengths include their multiple languages, cultures, and experiences—many migrant families are from different indigenous communities as well as different immigrant cultures.
- Schools and educators need to provide safe learning spaces within classrooms and throughout the school that promote the access for higher order, critical thinking as defined by Common Core State Standards.

Educational practices and characteristics that are socially just are a venue for fully supporting migrant students and their families. Providing high-quality migrant education programs at the local, state, and national level are a must if our migrant students are to have an opportunity to succeed in our nation's schools.

An NEA policy brief (2010) noted that general high-quality migrant education program characteristics include:

- A well-rounded curriculum that enhances cognitive, physical, health and nutrition, social and emotional domains of migrant students development;
- Small class sizes when appropriate to provide direct services with favorable teacher–student ratios, and possibly bilingual teachers or staff when available;
- Teachers and administrators who are caring and are knowledgeable of the migrant lifestyle and the languages and cultures of migrants, and are effectively trained to work with multiple populations of migrant students and their families;
- Ancillary services that meet the needs of migrant students such as;
  o Integrated migrant school-family and community partnerships so that migrant families can help their own children with school learning outcomes as well as opportunities for migrant families to increase their own educational attainment through English as a Second Language courses or citizenship courses;
  o Programs that address migrant student health, nutrition, and other family needs as part of a comprehensive network, and which are provided to all children;
  o Developing accountability measures in order to meet the needs of the migrant communities (National Education Association of the United States-Office of Minority Community Outreach, 2010).

In chapter 1, we discuss the importance of designing professional learning development for migrant education instructional programs that are grounded within a sociocultural context. The NEA brief further supports that notion. The following section in chapters 6–9 offer professional learning development strategies that are aligned with the Essential Element presented in the Esperanza County and Estación School District Story.

GOING DEEPER

This chapter discussed and described the Essential Element—Assessing Cultural Knowledge. The chapter drew from the rubric in Table 4.1, and focused on the Essential Element—Assessing Cultural Knowledge. This element guides educators and school teams to assess their cultural knowledge in working on behalf of and with students from migrant families and communities.

A case story from the hypothetical Esperanza County and Estación School District was introduced to provide illustrations of a school district that is a leader implementing culturally proficient educational practices, with emphasis on migrant students and their families.

The chapter provided critical, reflective, meditational, and dialogic questions to guide your and your colleagues' thinking about your own culture and your knowledge of your students' cultures. Lastly, we shared an example of a professional learning strategy designed to assess your cultural knowledge of self, of your colleagues, and about the community you serve.

Take a moment to think about your thinking with regard to topics discussed or described in this chapter. What key learning and insights surface for you? What assumptions about your migrant students were you holding on to prior to beginning this book? In what ways have these assumptions guided your teaching or leadership behaviors? What assumptions do you hold about migrant students? In what ways have these assumptions guided your decisions about nonformal leadership, curriculum, instruction, and assessment?

Reflection Activity

Now that you know what you know—and given that your assumptions have been revealed—what are you willing to do? What might it take to create a classroom, school, or district culture in support of migrant students? What assets do you, and your school or district, possess that supports you in this endeavor? What challenges or obstacles do you anticipate?

Dialogic Activity

Gather a group of like-minded colleagues to engage in a dialogue to reach shared understanding of *a school culture in support of migrant students performing at levels higher than ever before.* Continue the dialogue throughout small learning communities in the school or district or both. As a next step, discuss what might be some resources, strategies, and structures that could be developed and activated to support all learners, with particular emphasis on migrant students, their families, and their communities? As a final step, list one bold step you are willing to take; share those bold steps among members of your small learning community.

Chapter 6

Valuing Diversity Is Reflected in the Beliefs and Values You and Your School Hold and How You Share Those Beliefs and Values with Your Community

If we can get over our idea that wisdom is exclusive to certain people or groups, then our world expands dramatically.

—Dzogchen Ponlop (2010, p. 171)

GETTING CENTERED

Words related to being effective in educating children and youth from migratory families include "migrant," "migratory," "indigenous," "cultural," "diverse," and "equity." Imagine for a moment that a team of international educators is visiting schools across North America, and is visiting your classroom or school today. What might they see that would indicate how much you and your school value, in general, diversity and, in particular, migrant students and their families?

OPPORTUNITY TO JOURNAL

Once again, return to your journal to list and describe artifacts that visitors would see that demonstrate a value for diversity. What could be added to your curriculum and instructional program to further enhance a value for diversity? Are there questions that you and your colleagues should address to your school community even as you continue to demonstrate a value for diversity?

VALUING DIVERSITY

In chapter 5 we discussed the importance of Assessing Cultural Knowledge in arriving at the optimum point along the culturally proficient continuum, which is the point at which one or one's school is culturally competent. Becoming knowledgeable about the cultural and linguistic student populations in your school and community provides the basis for valuing the assets that cultural and linguistic diversity contributes to the school and the community. The challenge for us as educators is committing to learning about the varied experiences of immigrant migratory families, who are part of many indigenous cultures and speak different languages.

Being engaged in professional learning about migrant populations is the first of two steps in addressing educational access and achievement disparities. Professional learning focused on the cultures of migrant communities serves to demystify groups with whom we may have had limited contact in the past. Having learned knowledge about migrant communities, we are, then, prepared to align our and our schools' beliefs in high academic expectations, maintaining rigorous standards to expect positive outcomes for educating the Priority for Service migrant student population in our K–12 schools.

Inclusive belief systems regarding migrant students also extend to the Out-of School Youth and migrant farmworker families in our schools. Anderson (2014) notes that in schools "equity and diversity need to be embedded into the many facets of education: staff, pedagogical practices, communication, leadership, assessment, curriculum, and community engagement" (p. 12).

The highly respected organization Intercultural Development and Research Association (IDRA) provides a framework of six goals for educational equity and school reform that schools can use to achieve equitable educational and socially just outcomes. These six goals are used in this and subsequent chapters as a framework for working with migrant students and their families. Embedding these goals in school curriculum and school policies ensures valuing migrant students' language and cultural backgrounds. The six IDRA Educational Equity and Reform Goals are:

- *Goal 1: Comparably High Academic Achievement and Other Student Outcomes.* Data on academic achievement and other student outcomes that are disaggregated and analyzed reveals high comparable performance for all identifiable groups of learners, and achievement and performance gaps are virtually nonexistent.
- *Goal 2: Equitable Access and Inclusion.* There exists unobstructed entrance into, involvement and full participation of learners in schools, programs, and activities within those schools.

- *Goal 3: Equitable Treatment.* Patterns of interaction between individuals and within the school environment are characterized by acceptance, valuing, respect, support, safety, and security. This results in students feeling challenged to become invested in the pursuits of learning and excellence without fear of threat, humiliation, danger, or disregard.
- *Goal 4: Equitable Opportunity to Learn.* At minimum, the creation of learning opportunities so that every child, regardless of characteristics and identified needs, is presented with the challenge to reach high standards and are given the requisite pedagogical, social, emotional, and psychological supports to achieve the high standards of excellence that are established.
- *Goal 5: Equitable Resources.* Funding, staffing, and other resources for equity-based excellence are manifested in the existence of equitably assigned qualified staff, appropriate facilities, other environmental learning spaces, instructional hardware and software, instructional materials and equipment, and all other forms of instructional support, which are distributed in an equitable and fair manner such that the notion that all diverse learners must achieve high academic standards and other school outcomes becomes accepted by everyone.
- *Goal 6: Equitable Shared Accountability.* The assurance that all education stakeholders accept responsibility and hold themselves and each other responsible for every learner having full access to quality education, qualified teachers, challenging curriculum, full opportunity to learn, and appropriate, sufficient support for learning so they can achieve at excellent levels in academic and other student outcomes (www.idra.org).

Valuing diversity within the organizational culture of the school is the primary focus of this chapter. IDRA's Goal 2 (Equitable Access and Inclusion) and Goal 3 (Equitable Treatment) inform our examination of valuing diversity for both you the educator and your school or district as an organization. You will be guided to look inward to acknowledge and understand your own levels of valuing diversity when working with linguistically and culturally diverse migrant students and their families. Once you have facility with examining your own levels of valuing diversity, you are well equipped to assess the extent of your school's value for diversity.

Valuing diversity is the second Essential Element of Cultural Competence. As a culturally proficient educator, you and your colleagues

- Promote equitable access and inclusion type programs, strategies, resources, and policies in order to provide an unobstructed entrance into, involvement of, and full participation for linguistically and culturally diverse migrant students and their families in schools, programs and activities.

- Promote social justice and equitable treatment of migrant students and their families in the interaction between individuals and within an environment characterized by acceptance, valuing, respect, support, safety, and security such that migrant students feel challenged to become invested in the pursuits of learning and excellence without fear of threat, humiliation, danger, or disregard for who they are as migrant students.

OPPORTUNITY TO JOURNAL

Take a few moments to think about the migrant students in your school, district, or county and return to your journal to consider and respond to these prompts:

- In what ways do teachers, administrators, counselors, English-speaking parents, and community members perceive migrant students and their families?
- What might be some ways you and your colleagues can promote a socially just environment within the school as well as within society when working with linguistically and culturally diverse migrant students and their families?
- How might you demonstrate that you value diversity as a form of collaborating on common goals to share resources and engage in access opportunities to eliminate the achievement gap of migrant students?

Take a few moments to consider the questions posed in this section and in your journal describe the manner in which you and your colleagues value diversity as it relates to linguistically and culturally diverse migrant students and the families in your school community.

IDRA goals 2 and 3 when considered through the lens of Valuing Diversity provide educators and their schools relevant opportunities for professional learning. In this age of globalization, local and national expressions of valuing linguistic and cultural diversity is in our students' best interest.

VALUING DIVERSITY—TO PROVIDE
EQUITABLE ACCESS AND INCLUSION

Migrant students can achieve full participation, access, and inclusion to school services and resources when they know we value their languages and cultures. It is important that we make it clear to students, their parents, and community members that we welcome them in our schools and that we are dedicated to their being socially and academically successful. Being able to view, understand, and value as assets students' migrant communities and cultures is pivotal to our success as educators.

Many migrant students come to school speaking languages other than English, and in many cases speaking indigenous languages other than Spanish. In cases such as these, it creates a challenge for students in benefiting from school instruction, supportive resources, and a welcoming school culture. As inclusive educators, we know that valuing a child's language is the bridge to also valuing a child's culture and the culture of the child's family. Many migrant students speak English along with Spanish and their native indigenous language and, yet, they too often come to realize that their home languages are not being valued in U.S. society. The negative consequence of viewing students' lack of fluency in English as a deficit hinders students' pursuit of academic studies. This deficit approach is "despite the empirical evidence suggesting social, cognitive and psychological benefits of bilingualism" (Callahan & Gandara, 2015, p. 4).

In contrast with states that maintain English-only policies, there are also many states that support and value a child's language through the authorization of bilingual certification, often in multiple languages, for teachers. In those states, high school students receive a State Seal of Biliteracy on their high school diplomas. The seal verifies that students are proficient in both English and a second language. California alone had over 25,000 graduating seniors in 2014 who received the State Seal of Biliteracy (CDOE, 2015). Additionally, several states report an increasing interest among monolingual English-speaking families in dual-language education programs and those states have witnessed a marked increase in enrollment in dual immersion and bilingual programs in the past few years (Callahan & Gandara, 2015).

The uptick of interest in dual and bilingual programs raises important questions:

- Does this emergent value for language diversity accrue disproportionately to English-only-speaking students?
- How can we ensure that our migrant students benefit from this emergent value for language diversity on their path to bi- and trilingualism?

Our schools and society cannot afford to limit a value for multilingualism to traditionally well-served populations. It is imperative that schools demonstrate a value for diversity in language that is inclusive of the cultural fabric of each family, across the socioeconomic spectrum. The congruence of inclusive core values and culturally competent practices is basic to supporting our migrant students being academically successful and having full access to career and college readiness opportunities.

Dr. Sonia Nieto (2015) in her lecture at the University of San Diego's School of Leadership and Education Sciences noted that it is the valuing of students and families linguistic and cultural diversity that assists teachers in the development of stronger teacher and student relationships and, in turn, promotes success for all students. Engle and Gonzalez (2014) further accentuate Nieto's observation by noting that to be culturally competent as an instructional leader school leaders and their staffs must know and understand the cultural assets provided by the diverse communities they serve.

Engle and Gonzalez pose insightful questions to guide our ongoing professional inquiry in learning about migrant communities served by our schools:

• Where do migrant families come from?
• What are the different cultural groups represented in our school?
• What crops do they pick or follow in order to attain seasonal work?

Once inquiry is begun, as educators, we can research the cultural histories and traditions of our families. In so doing we benefit from knowing what brought many of the immigrant families to the United States and why they chose rural farmwork instead of urban employment. During this inquiry, related questions may reveal themselves, such as—Is their migration due to economic hardships in their home country? Is their migration due to religious marginalization or persecution? Have families been granted refugee status? What religious and nonreligious traditions do they celebrate?

In pursuing answers to questions such as these, we learn about culture through linguistic historical connections, we learn what languages our migrant communities speak. We learn about the indigenous languages that are spoken. Answers to questions such as these enable us to ensure that all students are able to see themselves and their families to be represented in the curriculum we teach.

As educational leaders, whether you are the formal leader of principal or a non-formal leader in the capacity of teacher or counselor, it is our collective responsibility to hold the school and classroom, the district, and the school board to an inclusive vision supported by core values that expresses the belief that all students can learn, including our migrant student. And, maybe even more importantly, we believe we are capable of learning how to educate students from migrant communities.

VALUING DIVERSITY IN ORDER TO ATTAIN EQUITABLE TREATMENT

Valuing diversity comes in many forms and patterns. IDRA's Educational Equity and School IDRA Reform Goal 2 proposes that equitable patterns of educator–student interaction are characterized by acceptance, respect, support, safety, and security. This is expected to ensure that students feel invested in the pursuit of learning and excellence and are free of fear, humiliation, danger, or disregard.

Valuing diversity in pursuit of professional learning and educator excellence can have a demonstrable effect on schools' instructional programs and practices. Migrant students' Individual Learning Plans (ILPs) or Migrant Education Program Comprehensive Needs Assessments or the State Service Delivery Plan provide excellent opportunities for planning and delivering professional learning. Effective planning takes into account research on effective schools and leadership as well as instructional practices that value student's sociocultural backgrounds. Inclusive practices focused on socially just and equitable practices lead to higher student achievement (Anderson, 2014; Quezada & Lindsey, 2012; Theoharis, 2007).

Similarly, student achievement is enhanced by "leaders who understand and recognize the importance of addressing diversity in all its forms as assets within the school community, rather than deficits and problems to be solved" (Lindsey & Lindsey, 2014, p. 37). In their professional learning communities, educators can use migrant students' ILPs to benchmark addressing and narrowing sociocultural inequities in the achievement of migrant students. Similarly, these learning communities can access school and community resources to identify and bridge College to Career Readiness opportunities in support of migrant students' successes.

VALUING DIVERSITY THROUGH FORGING FAMILY, SCHOOL, AND COMMUNITY PARTNERSHIPS AS CULTURAL ASSETS

When schools, families, and community groups work as partners to support learning, it leads to increased student academic achievement, families strengthened, and increased community support, therefore increasing parental involvement (Dantas & Manyak, 2010, Henderson & Mapp, 2002; Quezada, 2014, 2000). Epstein (2015) quite accurately notes,

> Today teachers have students from highly diverse families that differ in size and structure, in socioeconomic, racial, linguistic, cultural, and academic backgrounds, or all of the above. Teachers, counselors, administrators, and others in schools (e.g. nurses, office workers, food specialists) must know *how* to communicate with all students' families in positive ways to build mutual respect, trust, and appreciation of each other. (p. 1)

Migrant family work habits, of frequent moving to follow seasonal crops, makes forging school, makes family and community partnerships with schools to be even more important.

Quezada, Alexandrowicz, and Molina (2015) substitute the word "engagement" for "partnerships" as it is their experience that while schools often partner with families, the degree of true engagement with families varies. Too often engagement with lower socioeconomic, culturally diverse families is minimal when compared to engagement with families from more affluent communities.

In expressly valuing the diversity that migrant students and their families bring to school, educators can fully engage families in their children's education. Families representing language, cultural, and migratory realities different from the school too often participate at a minimal level in school activities. To continue to ignore migratory students in the educational process, professional learning communities can be a vehicle that brings together teachers, principals, and staff along with students, parents, and community partners to emphasize teamwork and school improvement to increase student learning opportunities (Epstein & Salinas, 2004). Epstein (2011) provides a framework of four new directions for organizing and conducting effective school, family, and community partnerships to fully engage families:

• Teamwork for Program Development,
• Goal-Linked Partnership Activities,
• Equitable in Outreach to All Families, and
• Evaluation of Program Quality and Results of Partnership Activities.

These four directions can assist educators to correctly value the cultural assets that migrant students and their families bring to schools.

Teamwork for Program Development—Effective program development requires a full team approach of educators (teachers, counselors, administrators, and other school personnel). Families and community partners develop comprehensive programs to meet the needs of migrant families and their children to fully engage students in goal-linked activities.

Migrant families that might not be at a school for an entire academic school year should not be precluded from leadership roles as it minimizes their roles and their voices will not be represented in planning activities. These activities can integrate both at-home and at-school activities. The activities might involve migrant farmworker parents in the construction and care of a school community garden or parents from the various indigenous cultural groups whose native and colorful clothing requires a particular stitch or sewing skills, or traditional cooking from their native regional and geographical areas. These can be activities for raising school funds where parents feel included and where limited educational resources are available in the schools where migrant students attend.

District (PAC), Region (RAC) and State (SPAC) Parent Advisory Councils provide leadership opportunities for presenting, modeling, and promoting culturally responsive techniques to meet the educational needs of linguistically and culturally diverse migrant student communities.

Goal-Linked Partnerships—It is important to engage families in planned activities that connect and contribute to improving the academic achievement of migrant students and which provide safe learning that fosters students developing positive attitudes toward school. If migrant students are lacking in literacy, math, or science skills it is important for educators and schools to plan family-friendly activities that may support them at home and which provide user-friendly activities where families may support their children even when parents and other family members may not speak English.

Jeynes' (2012) research study tells us that when schools and districts are engaged in goal-linked partnership practices student learning and motivation is enhanced, there is an increase in attendance, and student misbehavior is reduced. Goal-linked activities can be accomplished by engaging educators, the school, the district, and migrant families through migrant PACs, and community-based resources in a collaborative manner—that is, by engaging them as partners in the education of all students. Such structures often lead to strong migrant Regional Applications or District Service Agreements (DSA) or both.

Equitable Partnerships—Equity among parents, school, district, and community groups entails planning activities to reach all families—even those deemed to be traditional "hard to reach" families. Educators must demonstrate a will for engaging in partnerships. Educators need to devise mechanisms to provide implementation benchmarks and to assess the progress of family engagement programs. Educators can no longer afford to plan family engagement programs as a "single shot" activity to accommodate one group of parents. Activities such as these are especially important for educators as they allow them to assess their own cultural knowledge, as discussed in chapter 5. Genuine knowledge about our diverse communities provides opportunity to authentically express respect for the diversity within our schools.

Culturally proficient educators strive to support migrant farmworker families in meeting their need and right to be equitable partners with the communities and schools where their children attend. Epstein's four directions are to support you in developing and maintaining school-family and community partnerships as a way of communicating with migrant families and, maybe more importantly, will serve also as an equitable and culturally proficient manner for reaching all families.

OPPORTUNITY TO JOURNAL

Please consider the following questions supporting the context of equitable partnerships as you continue in this book. Take a few moments and return to your journal to record your thinking.

- In what ways can your school take advantage of the emergent synergy to be found in your linguistically and culturally diverse migrant families, their communities, and your school to enhance home, school, and community engagement so that stronger relationships and partnerships are fostered?
- In what ways can your school use professional learning communities to ensure that all migrant families represented in your school have equitable opportunities to be involved in their children's education?
- In what ways do you (or might you) reach out to and engage with linguistically and culturally diverse migrant families, who for the most part are regarded as "hard to reach families"?

In responding to questions throughout this book it is important to begin with: *What am I willing to do?* Given that Cultural Proficiency is an "inside-out" process, as an educator you must understand that Cultural Proficiency begins with ourselves as the educator(s) and moves outward in influences the manner in which we interact with our colleagues and the communities we serve. Equitable and socially just school-family, community partnership practices align educators' vision for equity through involving our migrant families and communities to focus on student achievement, to work with community partners, to communicate with migrant families, and to assure them they are an integral part of the educational and local learning community.

Positive behaviors displayed by school personnel serving our migrant populations result in families experiencing their migrant seasonal work, their cultures, and their languages being valued by the school and the larger community. Valuing the cultural assets that migrant students and their families bring to our schools builds our capacity to make any necessary shifts in being mindful of just and equitable outcomes for migrant students.

MINDFULNESS

The work of Cultural Proficiency is always about being intentional. Take a moment and look again at Table 2.1, The Cultural Proficiency Framework.

Each of the Four Tools is specific in its definition—the negative values inherent in the Barriers section, the positive core values that comprise the Guiding Principles of Cultural Proficiency, the range of behaviors explicit across the Continuum, and, in chapters 5–9, the Essential Elements serving as standards for ourselves and our schools.

After having read up until this point in the book, you most likely now recognize the Essential Elements of Cultural Proficiency to be the workhorses of the Four Tools of Cultural Proficiency. These are the "action words and behaviors" that we can employ in our daily actions and in school-wide planning.

Please be prepared for *planned redundancy* throughout the rest of this book. This is because the concept of the mindful, intentional use of the Essential Elements connects to a vision that embraces inclusivity (as expressed in the Guiding Principles of Cultural Proficiency). Expressing a Value for Diversity can be learned and actionable and, ultimately, becomes part of our DNA. So, let's build on your responses to the questions in the Mindfulness section of chapter 5. Please use these questions to guide your inside-out thinking and learning process. Be sure to have your journal available as you consider these questions.

My Inside-Out Learning Process

- When I'm by myself, to what degree do I value students and families from migratory communities?
- How might visitors to my classroom or school know my regard for migrant families? What would they see? What would they hear from me?
- In what ways might I question my regard for the culture of migratory families?
- What is in my classroom, or school, that demonstrates to students not from migrant communities, my value for migratory families? What do these students observe about my behavior that demonstrates a value for students from migrant communities?
- In what ways do these questions pique thoughts and feelings in me?

Facilitating OUR school's Inside-Out Learning Process About Valuing Diversity

- What are some ways my colleagues and I can learn about the migratory communities represented in our school community?
- What roadblocks, if any, may be obstructing our learning? Assuming roadblocks are identified, what can we do about lowering and removing them? What are we willing to do?

Facilitating My School's Inside-Out Learning Process for Valuing the Diversity in the Migrant Communities We Serve

- In what ways can our school community come to understand the extent to which we value the migrant communities we serve?
- If we are to move forward in serving our diverse communities equitably, in what ways do we, as a school, demonstrate a value for our migrant communities or students?

THE RUBRIC IN ACTION: VALUING DIVERSITY FOR INCLUSION AND SUPPORT OF MIGRANT EDUCATION STUDENTS, THEIR FAMILIES, AND THEIR COMMUNITIES

The Essential Element, Valuing Diversity, provides the opportunity for you and your school or district to express your high regard for all sectors of the diverse community you serve, expressly including students and their parents employed in migratory occupations.

Continuing the process begun in chapter 5 for examining one element of the rubric, let's examine how educators and their schools display how much they value diversity when working with students and their parents from migratory communities. Again, please use these two steps for initial study and use of the rubric:

Take a moment and refer back to chapter 4, Table 4.1, "Educators' Rubric for Inclusion and Support of Migrant Education Students, Their Families, and their Communities":

- You will notice when reading from left to right across any row of the rubric the developmental nature of moving from Cultural Destructiveness to Cultural Proficiency.
- Next look at Table 6.1. You will see that it presents only the Essential Element Valuing Diversity row from the rubric in chapter 4. Two things are important:
  - Table 6.1 presents the "affirmative" side of the rubric and omits the negative columns from the complete rubric. Undoubtedly, in your daily activities you will hear (and maybe even utter) some of the sentiments located under "Barriers." The rubric has been developed for the illustrations under Cultural Precompetence, Competence, and Proficiency to serve as suggestions to counter the negativity exemplified in the Cultural Destructiveness, Incapacity or Blindness columns.
  - When reading the illustrations for Cultural Precompetence, Competence, and Proficiency in Table 6.1, examine the adjectives and verbs, in particular the active voice and intentionality. Being mindful when

Table 6.1 Essential Element: Valuing Diversity for Inclusion and Support of Migrant Education Students, Their Families, and Their Communities

Essential Elements for Including and Supporting Migrant Students and their Families	Informed by Guiding Principles of Cultural Proficiency		
	Cultural Precompetence	Cultural Competence at Standard	Cultural Proficiency
Valuing Diversity—Extent to which educators value the linguistically and culturally diverse migrant students and their community. Migrant students and their families are inclusive of people and cultures with viewpoints and experiences different from educators for the benefit of the school and the community.	Educators acknowledge having limited knowledge about educational barriers of linguistically and culturally diverse migrant students due to their families' mobility, culture, and communities. Educator is committed to expanding the District Service Agreements (DSA) and/or Regional Applications (RA) by learning about the diverse culture of migrant families and communities they serve. Educator states willingness to learn about Family Biliteracy/School Readiness Programs, techniques and strategies that better serve linguistically and culturally diverse migrant students. Educator supports techniques that foster an understanding and trust among migrant students and their families. Employs instructional strategies that may be inconsistently applied among linguistically and culturally diverse migrant students due to their unique agricultural mobility.	Linguistically and culturally diverse migrant families and their communities are central to conversations, decision making and problem solving by the school, school district, and its community. Educators are part of the process including and engagement with the same content standards and core curriculum and engagement that results in higher academic achievement for migrant students. Lead and assist in Parent Advisory Councils and migrant parent conferences and meetings using linguistically and culturally appropriate communication or translations for verbal and written communication.	Using ILPs as benchmark, advance and develop mechanisms for creating a socially just school and society with particular emphasis on College to Career Readiness for Out-of-School Youth and Priority for Service Migrant Students who are linguistically and culturally diverse. Constantly engage in all aspects of your school community to collaborate on common goals and share educational and community resources. Engages in enhancing access of opportunity and eliminating achievement gaps, with particular attention paid to Out-of-School Youth and Priority for Service Migrant Students who are linguistically and culturally diverse.

reading the illustrations allows educators and their schools to engage in an "inside-out" process of intentional in personal and organizational change.

A Word of Caution. Leading and managing change, both personal and organizational, rarely proceeds in a linear fashion. Resistance to change is natural and normal, as you will hear it from colleagues who expect and comment that it is the students and their parents or guardians that are the ones who need to conform to prevalent school practices.

You may want to revisit the discussion in chapter 3 about how the Guiding Principles of Cultural Proficiency provide the moral framework of Cultural Proficiency and informs the right side of the rubric. You will see in the vignette that follows Ms. Luna, the middle school principal, models the "inside-out" approach to change in addressing the needs of long-term English-learning students. As you read the vignette pay particular attention to illustrations of progression along the rubric and how the moral framework for valuing diversity is represented in educators' words and actions.

VIGNETTE: ESPERANZA COUNTY AND PRÓXIMA ESTACIÓN SCHOOL DISTRICT

Following the meeting at the county office, Ms. Stone and Mr. Tamarit have called a meeting to examine programs targeting PF students who are in kindergarten through 12th grade. The goal is twofold: (a) horizontal—analyzes alignment between students' ILPs and program design; (b) vertical—the continuum of programs and their outcomes across grade level.

Ms. Stone—Assistant Superintendent:
Thank you for joining me today to initiate this dialogue on our policies and practices when working with PF migrant students. The county has identified the work we are currently doing with PF migrant students as an area to be revised, analyzed and redesigned. Mr. Tamarit, the room is yours. Please go ahead and provide the guidelines for our meeting.

Mr. Tamarit—Migrant Education Program Coordinator:
Thank you, Ms. Stone. In the past two weeks, I reviewed the last three District Service Agreements (DSA) submitted to the County Office. Reading through these documents, I observed the following: (a) our programs lack proper assessment tools to evaluate the outcomes of each program; (b) programs' outcomes are too broad; (c) programs do not reflect the diversity of our migrant students; and (d) most importantly, we are implementing over and over the same program without reflecting on their effectiveness and how these programs meet the

needs of our migrant students and more specifically the unique needs of our PF students.

Ms. Gutierrez—High School Teacher:

If I may ask, who wrote these DSAs? I was never asked to provide input. We just teach what we are asked to teach. Personally, I have not been trained to differentiate instruction when working with migrant students. I just teach. I would like to be better prepared but the reality is that I pretty much repeat what I am doing during my regular school day. Moreover, I do not know what PF means.

Ms. Zambrano—PAC Member:

We thought teachers were prepared to work with our children. How can our children be successful if nobody knows about migrant students?

Mr. Rose—Elementary School Teacher:

With all the respect, teachers know who their migrant students are. We tried our best but we have not been trained to meet the specific needs of migrant students. Listening to you all sounds like we have been teaching to students but not migrant students. I see this as a problem. The question is what can we do?

Ms. Castillo—PAC Member:

We need to work together. We parents are always informed about the programs but they do not ask us about our challenges. Each migrant student is different. Migrant students speaking different indigenous languages and have different needs. In our district, we have students who speak Triqui, Mixteco and others who speak Zapoteco. Do we value these languages? Or, do we assume every migrant student speaks Spanish?

Ms. Garmendia—Recruiter:

We gather this information—language spoken at home—when we recruit families. We do not know how this information is used.

Mr. Tamarit—Migrant Education Program Coordinator:

Thank you all for sharing your ideas. It is obvious that we have lots of work to do. Let me ask you some questions, what kind of training is needed to enhance our current practices? How can we develop a better understanding, awareness, and competence when working with migrant students? Do you have any ideas, suggestions to ensure we are including everyone in this process? And, a final question: why is it so important to meet the needs of all migrant students and in particular PF students?

Ms. Stone—Assistant Superintendent for Educational Instruction:

Thank you, Mr. Tamarit. We have an important task before us. I am here to support you in any way possible. I, personally, have to analyze my own assumptions and misconceptions on migrant students and their families. I am confident we can improve our practices but it will take having honest, difficult, and mindful dialogues. Please self-evaluate yourself and be ready to dialogue and actively listening to others. Looking forward to our next meeting. Thank you all for taking the time to being here with us. We need each one of you to make it happen: Best Practices, a Priority for All. Have a nice evening.

Guiding Questions

- What is, in your opinion, the rationale behind Mr. Tamarit's questions?
- Are these questions suggesting clear guidelines for moving forward?
- Can these questions guide the analysis of your own challenges when working with migrant students?
- Based on this vignette, what question(s) would you like to add to Mr. Tamarit's final statement?

PLANNING AND PROVIDING FOR PROFESSIONAL LEARNING WITH A SOCIALLY JUST FOCUS FOR EDUCATORS WHO TEACH MIGRANT STUDENTS

Authentic Professional Communities, Learning (PCLs) can be used and are disguised in various ways, for the most part it is the new buzzword and is too often treated as the new fad that substitutes the traditional staff development models. Shirley M. Hord (2009) describes a research-based attributes that qualifies as PLC's, they must provide the *Who*, the *Why*, and the *How*. By detailing the professional educators' involved addresses the (who), the reason why the learning that takes place the (why) and the code that the membership adheres to the (how).

Lindsey, Jungwirth, Pahl, and Lindsey rename Culturally Proficient Learning Communities as *Professional Communities, Learning* (PCLs) in order to highlight and raise the topic or theme of "culture" to the same level as organizational culture "on par with racial, ethnic, gender, social class, sexual orientation, faith, ableness, and language acquisition culture that abide in our schools" (Lindsey, Jungwirth, Pahl, & Lindsey, 2009, pp. 44–45). This notion of PCLs further support the content of this book and this section in particular as they are well aware that culturally proficient teachers and teaching is one of the most significant factors in student success.

They are also well aware that educators who value diversity are more apt to be more successful in building relationships with students and families from culturally and linguistic backgrounds. Well-planned culturally proficient PCLs can support educators in their efforts to gain knowledge about their new linguistically and culturally diverse migrant students, students' families, and the community they live in, which will enhance valuing diversity through holding a vision of social justice and equity for all students.

When culturally proficient PCLs are planned accordingly and conducted in a systematically and systemic process and, involve schools and community organization stakeholders (including the migrant community), they are then able to make them authentic in nature. They are able to facilitate an open and transparent dialogue that embraces migrant students' and their families' language and cultures as assets by which migrant student's educational experience and success is constructed. Therefore, effective leaders facilitate these PCLs sessions using specific procedures as well as cross-cultural and intercultural communication skills to support and drive decision making, problem resolving, and resource sharing in the best interest of migrant students, as well as all learners.

In turn, "participants in the PCL's engage in their own personal beliefs and values, the policies and practices of the school or district, the culture of one's community, and disaggregate data to create an instructional plan focused on improving achievement of all demographic groups" (Lindsey, Jungwirth, Pahl, & Lindsey, 2009). "Therefore, the need for school leaders to provide high quality, on-going, professional learning experiences focused on differentiated instruction and supported by coaching is critical for all teachers. The professional learning experiences must be designed to demonstrate a high value for the learners, their families, their languages and cultures and their communities" (Quezada, Lindsey & Lindsey, 2012, p. 82).

The Resource section following chapter 10 offers a professional learning strategy aligned with the Essential Elements from chapters 5 to 9 presented as the Esperanza County and Estación School District Case Story.

GOING DEEPER

The purpose of this chapter has been to describe the Essential Element of Valuing Diversity in the context of delivering appropriate education to students from migratory families. The Estación School District Case Story continues to provide illustrations for delivering Culturally Competent and Proficient education to our students who are from migratory families. The rubric presented in Table 4.1, Valuing Diversity, provides illustrations of practices in service of students and their migratory families.

As we conclude this chapter, you are provided opportunities to reflect on your own learning as well as questions or prompts to guide dialogic sessions with colleagues. You may want to return to your journal to take notes both for you own reflection and for planning dialogue with colleagues.

Reflection Activity

For this activity, you are asked to think of a particular context—your class-room, your wing of the building, or your school. You may want to close your eyes when responding to these prompts: Look around you and record what you see that demonstrates a value for students from migrant families. In what ways do students from migrant families see themselves in the formal and nonformal curriculum? How might students from nonmigrant families view their student peers from migrant families? What are you willing to do to demonstrate your value an equitable representation of migrant cultures?

Dialogic Activity

Convene a group of your colleagues, such as your PCL to develop a shared understanding of a professional learning environment invested in the cultures of migrant families. With shared understanding achieved, what might be some next steps in your collective professional learning?

Chapter 7

Managing the Dynamics of Difference to Make a Difference

When you have a conflict, that means that there are truths that have to be addressed on each side of the conflict. And when you have a conflict, then it's an educational process to try to resolve the conflict. And to resolve that, you have to get people on both sides of the conflict involved so that they can dialogue.

—Dolores Huerta

GETTING CENTERED

This, the third of the five essential elements, is about how conflict is managed. It may be that as you read the word "conflict" you had a visceral reaction, a desire to pull back. Please stay with us. First, conflict is natural and normal. The key is how we approach and deal with conflict. Second, let's try an analogy. Think of an interpersonal relationship that you admire—it might be a friendship, a marriage, a professional partnership, or it might be a blend of these. If the relationship is as successful as you deem it to be, there is near certainty that the people involved learned how to anticipate conflict and to deal with differences constructively. Second, interpersonal relationships that endure over time have shared mutual respect and shared values combined with a willingness and ability to communicate and to solve problems.

The major reason for our writing this book and, most likely for your picking it up to read, is either you or your school is hearing dissonant voices in the context of the education of students from migratory families. Acknowledging dissonance is an important first step in addressing conflict. Effective use of communication, problem-solving, and conflict resolution skills is predicated on being able to name the conflict. Our use of the journal throughout this book is for you and your colleagues to reflect on practice and to engage in dialogue for the purpose of understanding the *what,* and maybe the *why* of our behaviors. In this chapter, we focus on some of the *how*'s of communications and problem solving in the context of dealing with diverse student populations, with particular emphasis being paid to students from migratory families.

The basis for successfully navigating conflict in schools is best accomplished by having publicly shared values that are coupled with effective use of communication and problem-solving skills. Take a moment and return to the rubric in Table 4.1. Take particular note that the columns Precompetence, Competence, and Proficiency are under the broader column, Guiding Principles of Cultural Proficiency.

In practice, each of the behaviors embedded in all of the illustrations under those three columns are derived from the inclusive core values inherent to the Guiding Principles of Cultural Proficiency. (In stark contrast, the illustrations in the columns, Destructiveness, Incapacity, and Blindness are derived from the negative values embodied in barriers such as systemic oppression and unawareness of the need for schools to adapt to the student populations they have as opposed to the populations who used to be here or whom they wish they might have.)

OPPORTUNITY TO JOURNAL

Managing the dynamics of difference is about being personally and organizationally proactive. Let's take a few moments for you to think about your school and, in particular, your students, parents, and community members who are migratory. Consider this—at your next learning community meeting, grade-level or department meeting, or faculty meeting, someone suggests that the theme for this year's professional learning is Migrant Education. What might be some reactions from your colleagues? What are some of the comments that might be made? What might be some of the nonverbal responses? Would there be differences of opinion? How might differences of opinion among colleagues be handled? Return to your journal and take a few moments to record your thinking. In particular, note how participants deal with (or fail to deal with) differences of opinion and perspective.

MANAGING THE DYNAMICS OF DIFFERENCE

Migrant students and their families come from a vast array of cultures and speak a variety of indigenous languages such as Mixteco, Zapoteco, and Trique. Even these languages have dialects—for example, there's the Mixteco of Tezoatlán, the Mixteco of Yosondúa, and the Mizteco of Xochapa. These dialects coexist and identify each group as culturally and linguistically unique. Educators working with and learning from migrant communities must be aware and cognizant of this uniqueness and should know how the funds of linguistic and cultural knowledge can enrich and contextualize the programs and services provided to students and their families (Gay, 2000).

Appreciation and respect for migrant families comes from an inner dialogue in which educators reflect on their own biases and misconceptions. As Lisa Delpit (2005) points out, "We educators set out to teach, but how can we reach the worlds of others when we don't even know they exist?" (p. xxiv). The challenge is to find these worlds where migrant communities live, learn, and belong.

These worlds might exist and coexist within the communities where educators live; however, oftentimes, the migrant world remains anonymous and distant from the reality educators face on a daily basis. Educators might drive back and forth through highways that cross many agricultural fields where migrant families work to obtain an income. Yet once educators arrive at the school site or the community center, teaching and learning stand isolated from the fields on both sides of those highways. It takes a conscious and humble act of willingness to enrich teaching and learning with the migrant world. Seth M. Holmes (2013) summarizes the invisibleness of migrant workers in his 2014 Margaret Mead Award-winning book *Fresh Fruit, Broken Bodies*:

> Early in my fieldwork, I began to notice the segregation of workers in U.S. agriculture into a hierarchy of perceived ethnicity and citizenship. I observed economic inequalities and social hierarchies producing displacement, migration, sickness, and suffering. . . . I noticed several ways in which social and health inequalities had become considered normal, natural, and justified. I became discouraged by what appeared to be a depressing situation without any possibility for change. (p. 182)

The Educators' Rubric for Inclusion and Support of Migrant Students, Their Families, and Their Communities, Table 4.1, illustrates how and why those educators who suppress or avoid the enrichment of curricula and services with the lives and experiences of migrant students their families and their communities are displaying unresponsive or indifferent attitudes about the culturally and linguistically diverse migrant families as they move from city to city or from state to state. Further, these practices—suppression and avoidance—deny the value of all the memories and stories migrant families own as part of their identity and their persona. Hooks (2008), when analyzing the power of memories, states: "The past [is] a resource that can serve as a foundation for us to revision and renew our commitment to the present, to making a world where all people can live [and learn] fully and well, where everyone can belong" (p. 5).

Culturally proficient educators encourage and lead conversations around the memories and experiences migrant communities bring to the programs and services designed and implemented by MEOs. Moreover, they appreciate the value of such memories and stories and rise as advocates to defend and validate cultural and linguistic diversity.

MANAGING DIFFERENCE: EXPERIENCING MIGRANT STUDENTS' LIVES

Working with migrant communities calls for a specific set of skills from which educators draw their ability to connect and contextualize their practices. Oftentimes, educators label migrant students as English learners or immigrant students or both. Though these labels may fit a number of migrant students, they hide the fact that migrant students face additional and unique challenges—high mobility, lack of sense of belonging, and anonymization—that educators need to examine to ensure programs and service meet the needs of all these students.

This examination begins by recognizing the differences between the life lived by the educator, the experiences migrant students and their families go through, and the knowledge and skills targeted in the migrant education programs. Identifying these differences is a challenging task. Further, it calls for educators to compare the world in which they live with the world and the reality migrant students and their families confront every day.

Culturally proficient educators challenge themselves by positively engaging with the reality experienced by migrant students and their families. As Linksy and Heifetz (2002) explain, "No one learns only by staring in the mirror. We all learn—and are sometimes transformed—by encountering differences that challenge our own experience and assumptions" (p. 101). These differences are discussed in inclusive spaces where educators, students, and families cooperatively construct a *We* space, a space equally built and owned by students, families, and personnel working in migrant education programs. Rodríguez-Valls and Ponce (2013), in their analysis of migrant education programs, define the *We* space as a place where identity is a twofold concept. Identity "(a) represents the unique and distinct knowledge each [migrant] student produces and acquires and (b) is the collective educational gain all the participants [students, parents and educators] build and share and the end of the learning process" (p. 12).

The next step is to extend the *We* space from the individual classroom where teachers and migrant students teach and learn from each other to an inclusive and broader educational environment. Further, the *We* space developed by a single educator should be cohesive and coherent with other *We* spaces built by their colleagues. At this point managing differences becomes a communal task. Van Baalen & Moratis (2012) state that this task "is not a clear-cut and a rather complex task. It depends on the number and the nature of the stakeholders (those who are affected by or have an interest on the activities and existence) of the [school site]" (p. 157). The next section examines how educators working within the same school district manage their differences to effectively work with and learn from migrant students and their families.

MANAGING THE DIFFERENCE: FROM SCHOOL DISTRICTS TO MIGRANT STUDENTS AND THEIR FAMILIES

In the last 20 years, McCollum and García (1996), Gibson & Bejinez (2002), Spaulding, Carolino & Amen (2004), Gibson & Hidalgo (2009), and Rodríguez-Valls, Kofford & Morales (2012) have analyzed the challenges educators face in the development of successful and effective migrant education programs. Among the challenges identified in these studies, there are three that are common: (1) the insufficient cohesiveness across the different agencies attempting to help students and families overcome the lack of belonging, anonymization, and high mobility; (2) the dearth of preparation among personnel to understand the unique needs of migrants students and their families; and (3) the lack of appropriate programs and assessment tools designed specifically to meet, evaluate, and support the academic and social success of migrant students and their families.

The previous section described how each educator manages the differences between their reality and the migrant world, and how effective practices at the school district level must assemble all the assets each educator brings to the migrant programs. Regardless if teachers working in the same school design an after-school program focusing on study skills, or teachers from different schools working together in a summer program with an emphasis on how science, technology, engineering, art, and mathematics they are connected to the migrant community, all educators must recognize that they have a common goal. As Epstein (2011) underlines in her work on educational partnerships: educators and staff must "recognize shared responsibilities of home, school and [migrant] community for [migrant] children's learning and development"

(p. 11). Therefore, developing effective practices when working with migrant students calls for a cohesive effort from school district personnel.

A key to building coherence and consistency in migrant education programs is having a solid leadership group that manages the pedagogical differences that may exist among teachers and staff. To recognize, value, and manage such differences, administrators must create spaces—via professional development—in which all personnel involved in migrant education programs examine their individual pedagogies and approaches.

The role administrators have while leading the effort in the different school districts is pivotal. The strength and effectiveness of programs require what Linsky and Heifetz (2002) define as dangerous, but needed, dialogues where the "values, beliefs, or habits of a lifetime" (p. 12) of individuals are being questioned and where each person participating in these dialogues feels empowered to "tell people what they need to hear rather than what they want to hear" (p. 12).

In Table 7.1 a culturally proficient educator is defined as the one who has the courage to lead conversations even though others may challenge her or his thoughts. In addition, the culturally proficient educator takes steps that may not be liked but are deemed necessary to provide the best service to migrant students and their families. The culturally proficient educator recognizes the need for linking goals, objectives, and outcomes across practices and from all educators.

As Palmer points out, "Good teachers possess a capacity for connectedness. They are able to weave a complex web of connection among themselves, their subjects and their students so that student can learn to weave a world for themselves" (p. 11). If we were to rephrase Palmer's thoughts, we would say that educators working in migrant education programs must be able to meet the needs of all migrant students and families. In doing so, they end the societal and educational injustices faced by migrant communities. They are problem solvers willing to mediate, knowing that "although you [they] may see with clarity and passion a promising future of progress and gain, people will see with equal passion the losses you [they] are asking them to sustain" (Linsky & Heifetz, 2002, p. 12).

One more factor that differentiates culturally proficient educators from those who perpetuate practices without reflection, is their capacity to lead the way on adaptive challenges, which Heiftz (2010) defines as those in which there "is a problem situation for which solutions lie outside the current way of operating. . . . An adaptive challenge is created by a gap between a desired state and reality that cannot be closed using existing approaches alone" (p. 73).

In the next section you will read a vignette depicting a meeting in which participants present their views on migrant education programs. Using the ideas shared in the previous two sections, analyze what the participants are saying and how they are reacting and responding to what others are saying. As you read the dialogue, reflect on which level of the rubric (Managing the Dynamics of Difference) you would place each participant. Visualize yourself in the dialogue and how you would respond if you were to participate in the dialogue. The goal is to evaluate yourself as an educator who manages differences to create a common goal when working with migrant students and their families.

MINDFULNESS

Consistent with the previous two chapters, the questions that follow are designed to provide you and your colleagues an opportunity to think about what's possible in your school context and to be flexible in your learning. Return to your journal when appropriate to record your reflections and the key points made during conversations with colleagues.

MY INSIDE-OUT LEARNING PROCESS

- How comfortable am I with my conflict resolution skills? What more do I want to learn about managing the dynamics of difference involved in school-based groups that support migrant students and their families?
- As I reflect on my thoughts and experiences about migrant groups in our country, what are some issues I still need to explore? How might I proceed to learn further about these issues? In what ways might these unresolved issues impact my effectiveness as an educator?
- What might be my next steps?

Facilitating OUR School's Inside-Out Learning Process about Managing the Dynamics of Difference

- In what ways do migrant students experience our school differently from nonmigratory students?
- What could be our faculty's next steps to constructively address these differences? What data might we need? What knowledge and skills might we need?
- In what ways might the Guiding Principles of Cultural Proficiency, when expressly inclusive of the migrant experience, inform our school's mission, vision, and core values?

**Facilitating My School's Inside-Out Learning Process
about Managing the Dynamics of Difference with the
Communities We Serve**

- Now that I know what I have learned thus far in this book, in what ways
  does this knowledge support my continued learning about the diverse
  nature of our community?
- With our school's vision, mission and core values inclusive of the migrant
  experience, in what ways can we best serve our students from migrant
  families?
- What might be some of the benchmarks to illustrate improvements in
  addressing the educational needs of all students, but especially students
  from migratory families?

THE RUBRIC IN ACTION: MANAGING THE
DYNAMICS OF DIFFERENCE FOR INCLUSION AND
SUPPORT OF MIGRANT EDUCATION STUDENTS,
THEIR FAMILIES, AND THEIR COMMUNITIES

Very importantly, the "Essential Element" "Managing the Dynamics of Difference" provides opportunity to explore our school's organizational culture.
This element deepens the *inside-out process* in such a way that we often
uncover and examine embedded assumptions that are discomforting. Please
know that in this context discomfort may be an indicator of being on the
verge of deeper learning.

Most likely what will be revealed are policies and practices that are not
equitable and which must be changed so as to be inclusive. The acid test of
successful self-examination is the realization that it is not the students and
their parents or guardians who need to conform to the school; instead, it is
the responsibility of the school to incorporate the assets of the migrant communities into the school culture so as to enhance the learning opportunities
of adults and students. Through embracing conflict as something natural and
normal, all sectors of the school community benefit. Table 7.1 is designed to
extend and deepen your knowledge and facility with the Essential Elements
as action words in your journey to becoming a culturally proficient educator.
Consider these steps as you review the rubric and as you pay specific attention to the Essential Element, Managing the Dynamics of Difference:

- Take a few moments and turn back to Table 4.1 and examine Educators'
  Rubric for Inclusion and Support of Migrant Education Students, Their
  Families, and Their Communities.

Table 7.1 Essential Element: Managing the Dynamics of Difference for Inclusion and Support of Migrant Education Students, Their Families, and Their Communities

Essential Elements for Including and Supporting Migrant Students and Their Families	Informed by Guiding Principles of Cultural Proficiency		
	Cultural Precompetence	*Cultural Competence at Standard*	*Cultural Proficiency*
Managing the Dynamics of Difference— Extent to which educators use problem-solving and conflict resolution strategies as ways to be inclusive of multiple perspectives and to teach others about the dynamics of cultures in contact with one another.	Participate in developing Family Biliteracy/School Readiness Programs as part of the Regional Applications (RA) or District Service Agreements (DSA) and skills in problem-solving and conflict resolution strategies that are culturally responsive to migrant groups. Gather and evaluate Family Biliteracy/School Readiness Programs as part of the Regional Applications (RA) or District Service Agreements (DSA), and academic assessments, as well as placement information on some migrant students that may be unreliable and/or inconsistent. Weigh the associated benefits and risks to migrant students by examining programs such as Family Biliteracy/School Readiness Programs as part of the Regional Applications (RA) or District Service Agreements (DSA) of action and weigh the associated benefits and risks.	Encourage and lead conversations that emerge into diverse opinions and perspectives across cultures and viewpoints as a usual and ordinary process within your school and the linguistically and culturally diverse migrant community it serves. When facilitating conversations, anticipate and challenge resistance; then, take measures that may not be well-liked but are deemed necessary in addressing the needs of a full range of migrant students within the linguistically and culturally diverse migrant communities your school serves.	Using ILP as benchmark, resolve matters that arise among migrant cultural groups and families to fully understand about the school and community educational, and societal injustices experienced by Out-of-School Youth and Priority for Service Migrant Students who are linguistically and culturally diverse. Work with Parent Advisory Councils and linguistically and culturally diverse migrant communities served by the school in a vigorous way to decipher and solve issues that are prevalent with Out-of-School Youth and Priority for Service Migrant Students and migrant communities served.

Source: Adapted from Reyes L. Quezada, Delores B. Lindsey, & Randall B. Lindsey (2012). *Cultural Proficiency Practice-Educators Supporting English Learning Students.* Thousand Oaks, CA: Corwin.

- As you have done previously, notice when reading from left to right across the rubric the manner in which language shifts from Cultural Destructiveness to Cultural Proficiency.
- Now, read Table 7.1. You will see Table 7.1 of the rubric, the Essential Element, Managing the Dynamics of Difference for Inclusion and Support of Migrant Students.
  - This table includes only the "positive" side of the rubric, namely Cultural Precompetence, Cultural Competence, and Cultural Proficiency. By reading to this point in the book, you recognize that the behaviors, policies, and practices located on the left side of the rubric exist in society and too often in our schools. It is important to acknowledge that negatives exist but the emphasis here is when hearing or otherwise experiencing negatives, the right side of the rubric provides suggested comments or practices for you and your colleagues. Viewing these oppositional sides of the rubric deepens understanding of the *inside-out* nature of Cultural Proficiency and facilitates being intentional in leading and fostering personal and organizational change, in this case for meeting the academic and social needs of students from migratory families.

Now that you have the understanding and facility with three of the Essential Elements, we return to our case story with the Próxima Estación School District.

PRÓXIMA ESTACIÓN SCHOOL DISTRICT CASE STORY: SCHOOLS WITHIN THE DISTRICT

This vignette illustrates the various views school principals have on migrant education and how some of these views weaken the effectiveness of both programs and services provided to migrant students and their families.

The cohesiveness of the design, implementation, and evaluation of migrant programs is key to ensuring migrant students and their families are equipped with the right tools to: (a) overcome the lack of belonging when they arrive at a new school district; (b) become active and present members of the school community; and (c) successfully navigate the educational system.

Participants:

Ms. Stone—Assistant Superintendent for Educational Instruction
Mr. Zarzoso—Superintendent at Próxima Estación School District
Mr. Tamarit—Migrant Education Program Coordinator
Mr. Zambrano—PAC member

Dr. Reed, Principal—Camino Elementary School
Ms. Sol, Principal—Greenfield Middle School
Mr. Soto, Principal—Adelante High School
Mrs. Del Rio—Counselor, Adelante High School
Ms. Gutierrez—High School Teacher

Mr. Rose—Elementary School Teacher:
As part of the series of meetings scheduled to evaluate programs targeting PF students, Ms. Stone has invited superintendents, school principals, teachers, counselors, and Regional Academic Coordinator members to analyze the cohesiveness of programs and services across the school district

Ms. Stone—Assistant Superintendent for Educational Instruction:
Thanks for joining us in our second meeting focusing on the programs and services we as school district offer to PF migrant students and their families. I would like to remind you that the Board at the County Office has identified this area as a key element when refining and developing future programs. I am fully aware that there are different views in terms on program design, implementation and evaluation; however, our goal is to strengthen the cohesiveness, effectiveness and outcomes of our programs and services. And now, I would like to thank you, Mr. Zarzoso, for being with us today.

Mr. Zarzoso—Superintendent at Próxima Estación School District:
Thank you, Ms. Stone. We at Próxima Estación School District value the support the County Office is always providing us when working with migrant students. We take our jobs with a great deal of responsibility. Moreover, we feel that we provide high quality services to this population. However, there is always room for improvement. As Ms. Stone said, our goal today is to learn from each other and to come up with ideas that will help us to meet the needs of our PF migrant students.

Mr. Tamarit—Migrant Education Program Coordinator:
Thank you, Ms. Stone and Mr. Zarzoso. In the past couple of weeks, I talked with all the school principals in our school district to gather their ideas and opinions on the programs and services we are currently offering to PF migrant students and their families. Talking with the school principals, I realized we have various understandings on who our migrant students are and the needs they have. Although variances always enrich dialogue, it seems to me that in some cases migrant students are somehow invisible, we do not really know who they are; therefore, their needs are not being met.

Mr. Soto—Principal, Adelante High School:
Wait a minute, wait a minute. Are you saying that we do not know who our migrant students are? Every year, you gave us the list with the migrant students

in our schools. We are implementing the programs you prescribe to us. What else is expected from us?

Mr. Tamarit—Migrant Education Program Coordinator:
With all the respect Mr. Soto, what I implied is that the way we are serving our PF migrant students could be enhanced if we better understand their needs.

Ms. Sol—Principal, Greenfield Middle School:
May I interject before you keep talking? Your words sound a little bit accusatory. Are you telling us that we need to change the way we work with migrant students? I know my community and I can tell you who the Greenfield students are. I thought that when you talked with us and today's meeting was to refine our practices, not to question our different management styles and our awareness on who our students are.

Ms. Stone—Assistant Superintendent for Educational Instruction:
Ms. Sol, you are right. We are here to discuss our current practices and to strengthen the cohesiveness of our practices. After Mr. Tamarit talked with all the principals, Mr. Zarzoso, Mr. Tamarit and I had a meeting to debrief on the conversations he had with all the principals. It was evident to all of us that we need to rethink and revise our practices when working with PF migrant students.

Dr. Reed—Principal, Camino Elementary School:
Ms. Stone, could you please be more specific on what you meant by "it was evident that we need to revise our practices"?

Mr. Zarzoso—Superintendent at Próxima Estación School District:
Ms. Stone, do you mind if I answer Dr. Reed's question?

Ms. Stone—Assistant Superintendent for Educational Instruction:
Please, go ahead.

Mr. Zarzoso—Superintendent at Próxima Estación School District:
Dr. Reed, we value and respect how you and all the school principals work with your teams to meet the needs of PF migrant students. The purpose of our meeting today is not to question how you and your colleagues manage your schools. Our goal is to strengthen the cohesiveness of our programs. We listen and learn from each other. I am confident we can meet the expectations we have at the school district as well as the ones set by the County Office. If you do not mind, I would like to hear from the teachers.

Ms. Gutierrez—High School Teacher:
Thank you Mr. Zarzoso. Personally, I need specific examples on these areas for improvement. We are trying our best to meet the needs of migrant

students but we do not have enough time. Each teacher tries her/his best. Truth is, we need more support and training to increase our awareness and skills to better serve migrant students. I am here to share and to learn from each other. I would like to go back to my school with a set of strategies and ideas.

Mrs. Del Rio—Counselor, Adelante High School:

I agree with Ms. Gutierrez, we are working really hard to support migrant students and their families. But, the reality is that with so many priorities sometimes we cannot offer what they need. We need a consistent and cohesive structure to unify our practices. As per now, each one of us battles on her/ his own. There is not a common understanding on what effectiveness and excellence means when working with migrant students. We work isolated from each other, perhaps because we do not know how to understand and support others.

Mr. Zambrano—PAC member:

I believe you all have the same goal: to better serve our families. I am not sure if you understand that within migrant, there are thousands of us and each one of is unique and different.

Ms. Stone—Assistant Superintendent for Educational Instruction:

This is a good start. The key is how, when, why and to whom we value, respect and learn from.

OPPORTUNITY TO JOURNAL

As you think about the conversation among these Próxima Estación educators, take a few moments to reflect on the conversation and respond to the following questions. Use your journal to record your thinking and questions that are surfacing for you.

- What are some of the views expressed in the conversation?
- How did Mr. Tamarit respond to what the principals said?
- What might have been other strategies group members could have used to refocus the conversation?
- Based on this dialogue, where might you locate each participant on the rubric? What evidence would you indicates supports your assessment?
- What are the next steps to be followed after this meeting?

GOING DEEPER

Congratulations, you are proceeding well on your cultural proficiency journey. The rubric illustrates clear choices for us and for our schools and districts. If we dwell in the realm of negative behaviors, policies, and practices inherent in Cultural Destructiveness, Cultural Incapacity, and Cultural Blindness, we are informed and maintained by negative core values of systemic oppression, unawareness of the need for schools to adapt in ways that embraces the assets inherent in migrant worker cultures, and schools oftentimes being resistant to change. However, if we choose to be proactive with Cultural Precompetence, Cultural Competence, and Cultural Proficiency, we embrace the cultures of migrant communities as assets on which to build their educational experience.

Reflection Activity

You are now at the "now that you know what you know" part of the inside-out journey of Cultural Proficiency. So, let's continue! You have begun to surface and examine your assumptions about people from migrant communities; so, what are you willing to do? What are you willing to do to deepen your own learning? What might you need to do in developing a culture of inclusion for students from migrant communities into the mainstream of your school?

Dialogic Activity

Every journey begins with a single step is a maxim undoubtedly familiar to all. Engage your colleagues to develop a shared understanding in developing an inclusive professional learning program that is expressly inclusive of migrant communities and cultures. The desired outcome of this program would be to manage the dynamics of difference in your school and across the district that would have students from migrant communities involved socially and academically to the extent that they would be on par with all other students.

As you initiate and continue the dialogue, pay particular attention to areas of agreement and zones of tension. The zones of tension may be the starting points of deeper learning that will result in you (and the professional community you are part of) becoming ever more successful with students from migrant communities.

Chapter 8

Adapting to the Diversity as a Team in the Schools and Communities We Serve

In the *this as that*, neither the *this* nor the *that* is given forthwith, outside of the discourse.

—Émmanuel Lévinas (2005, p. 13)

GETTING CENTERED

Educators play diverse roles. These include the role of teachers, counselors, aides, administrators, directors, and specialists. Though each of these roles is distinct, they share a common focus—the education of students. The diverse roles played by educators, however, challenge effective communication, particularly when these roles have to be played while dealing with diverse student populations.

In this chapter we proceed to the fourth Essential Element—Adapting to Diversity. Our role as educators is to support the notion of the importance of communication as we work together to design and deliver effective, inclusive educational opportunities to our students.

ADAPTING TO DIVERSITY AS AN EDUCATOR, A SCHOOL LEADER, AND AS A MEMBER OF THE COMMUNITY WE LIVE IN

The Cultural Proficiency Continuum provides a range of viewpoints to inform our *inside-out approach* toward being reflective in planning for our personal and organizational growth. It begins by renewing and invigorating

OPPORTUNITY TO JOURNAL

Given the various roles played by educators, the diversity seen in student populations as well as in parents, guardians, and members of your community, in what ways do you learn about others' views, experiences, and preferences? In what ways do you learn about their cultures? How do you communicate, both within your school and across the community served by your school? In what ways would you like to improve communication? What steps are you willing to take to improve communication? Please turn to your journal and record your thinking. Your responses will frame the manner in which you benefit from this chapter.

Adapting the benefits of diversity that migratory families have and bring to our schools involves ourselves as educators being actively engaged in our own learning journey and learning about linguistic and culturally diverse migrant families and communities. Our continuous professional learning involves the manner in which we as educators respond to societal and academic inequities that confront migrant students, their families, and communities in classrooms, schools, and in the context of the larger community. By focusing on our own process of adapting to diversity, we deepen our understanding of the extent to which cultural knowledge is foundational to inclusive education being based in a moral commitment. It is the *inside-out* process of commitment to inclusivity of individual educator values and school policies that give rise to worthwhile goals of equitable educational and socially just outcomes.

our commitment to support more effectively our migrant students and their families. Culturally proficient educators must approach recent educational reform initiatives such as No Child Left Behind, Race to the Top, Common Core, and the new Every Student Succeed Act of 2015 (DOE, 2015) in ways that guarantee a focus on ethnically diverse student populations.

Although there are safeguards in the Every Student Succeed, Act of 2015 to array and analyze access and achievement data relative to low-income students, students of color, and English learners (http://edtrust.org/wp-content/uploads/2014/09/Detailed-ESSA-Overview.pdf), it is our responsibility as educators to address our and our colleagues' attitudes and behaviors in working with and educating linguistically and culturally diverse migrant students and families. It is our duty to challenge historical deficit-based attitudes that remain deeply embedded and integrated in our educator, school, and organizational practices. As educators we must adapt to asset-based approaches that foster our continuous learning, embracing, and embedding equitable and socially just instructional and institutional policies and practices.

In chapter 6 we introduced two of IDRA's Educational Reform Goals, *Equitable Access and Inclusion* and *Equitable Treatment*. This chapter focuses on *Goal 6: Equitable Shared Accountability* to frame our discussion of how to adapt to diversity. The intent of the goal is to assure that all education stakeholders hold themselves and one another responsible for every learner having full access to quality education, qualified teachers, a challenging curriculum, and full opportunity to learn. Taken together, these educator commitments provide appropriate, sufficient support for learning so that students can achieve high academic and social outcomes (www.idra.org).

The challenge we face as educators is holding our state and local leaders accountable for making equity-based and socially just decisions to provide resources, support, and interventions to schools and students in most need, in many cases schools with high migrant students, particularly rural populations.

Funds of Knowledge as a Conceptual Framework for Inclusion Based in Educator Adaptation

Educators and education stakeholders must hold themselves and others responsible for every learner, including students from migratory families, having full access to quality education. UNESCO's International Taskforce on Teachers For Education for All (http://www.teachersforefa.unesco.org/v2/index.php/en/) holds that every child deserves a quality teacher. There is no exception for migrant students.

Educational access and academic achievement gaps among migrant students and their peers persist. Too often educational programs for migrant students were developed for students who were at the school a generation ago. Instead what is needed are innovative programs and curricula that are developed for our current migrant students, many of whom are from varied indigenous groups. By providing outdated educational programs, we risk extending deficit-based assumptions about the capabilities of today's migrant students and families. Further, the needs of the migrant students today differ from those of migrant students from 20 years ago. The key traits defining a migrant student—high mobility, lack of belonging, and anonymization—differ in nature as these three characteristics were framed during the last three decades.

Adapting to Diversity is an Essential Element of the Cultural Proficiency's *inside-out* approach to change. It is situated in ways that meets the educational needs of this new generation of migrant students and their families. For too long our migrant students and their families have had to blindly adapt to the norms of our schools and the dominant culture and this most often leads to a widening academic achievement gap.

The respected researcher Jim Cummins (2000) refers to this approach or way of thinking as an attitude "to ensure students remain within predetermined cultural and intellectual boundaries" (p. 284). This paradigm must be challenged as "it promotes the prevailing assumption that it is only students from marginalized groups and their families who should conform in order to be successful at school."

Similarly, Nieto (2010) notes that it is teachers and schools who need to change (p. 101). Bartolome (2008) observed that educators, particularly teachers, "possess tremendous agency to challenge and transform harmful ideologies" (p. xxi). As educators, we have the capacity to adapt and change in ways that support our students' learning when we have the will to learn how their cultures support their learning (Quezada, Lindsey, & Lindsey, 2012).

There are many ways we as educators can adapt to diversity. We can commit to learning or using the languages and cultures of the migrant communities being served by our schools. Learning and integrating the cultural knowledge, language abilities, customs, and practices in both curriculum and program development is a way to get to the core of the funds of knowledge, and value them as important resources that migrant students and their families bring to our schools (Gonzalez, Moll, & Amanti, 2005).

Banks and Park (2010) frame adapting to diversity to be a shift in a "cultural paradigm" in thinking about ethnic minority students from a negative view to an "assets-based perspective" that transcends the often-prevalent deficit views of migrant students and their families and other ethnic minority students. As educators we commit to professionally, personally, and organizationally taking the time to learn what is needed to ensure the academic and personal or social success of our linguistically and culturally diverse migrant student populations. The reason being is that the concept of funds of knowledge supports the notion of the importance that we as educators need to know about the students we serve "culturally (which) is not the same as knowing them psychologically" (Penetito, 2001, p. 20).

Individual schools taking steps to adapting to diversity is an important beginning, but this is not sufficient. Entire districts and county and state offices need to support migrant education programs so they may systemically address and close education, academic, language, and cultural gaps. As we adapt to the demographic diversity of the new generation of migrant students, we will need to be more vigilant.

The global refugee crisis from the East, in particular Syria, Iraq, Afghanistan, and Central America, are bringing in new students to our nation's schools as well as having an impact on many European Union nations. These students will have different cultural and linguistic needs as well as learning styles, and cultural traditions. As educators we will need to commit resources that support the professional development of educators so that they are equipped with practices that will be effective with linguistically and culturally diverse migrant students and their communities.

Hogg's (2011–2012) extensive literature review on "funds of knowledge" asserts that it is the intersection of six types of conceptual framework theories that may be used by educators can also be used in planning curriculum for migrant students and for increasing the social and cultural effectiveness of educators and their schools. Hogg (2011–2012) identifies sociocultural learning theory, critical theory, hybridity theory, systems theory and difference theory of caring sociocultural theory, critical theory and difference theory of caring can have a direct application on the Essential Element of Adapting to Diversity.

Sociocultural Theory

Sociocultural theory supports the notion that learning takes places as a result of authentic and genuine interactions with others. As educators, we need to form a sociocultural process that activates migrant students' prior knowledge and work; after all, many of our current migrant student populations represent many indigenous communities, therefore, bringing challenges as well as sociocultural assets. We also need to employ those who have the expertise and knowledge to better serve our students. As educators, we not only need to be experts on our own content, but we also need to engage in academic discourse to make academic connections with students so they too may become experts of their own knowledge. The hope is to have migrant students form a stronger identity.

What can we do as educators? We can begin by adapting to diversity by valuing and validating the knowledge and skills that migrant students bring to our classrooms as well as embracing the knowledge and expertise that their families bring to our schools. We must develop migrant students skills so they may use those skills as cultural tools for increasing academic achievement in all the content areas—language arts, mathematics, social studies, science, art, music,—as well as develop their college to career awareness as they transition from grade level to grade level (Moll, 1992).

We must ensure that we authentically integrate students' and their families' daily experiences into the curriculum. This means integrating into the curriculum knowledge related to the farms the families of migrant students work on, the types of crops the families harvest, the weather they encounter, the living conditions they have to live by—not from a deficit model, but from our framework of "caring and embracing." At the secondary school level, migrant students need to be provided opportunities to participate in apprenticeships to gain educational and career experiences they may not have had due to the mobility of their families' seasonal employment.

These situated learning apprenticeships can be structures like Communities of Practice (Lave & Wengner, 1991) based on the support and needs of the migrant students being served by a particular school district or by the county migrant education program. In this approach, both the community members and the migrant students assume their own respective expert roles and share the knowledge and perspectives they bring.

Critical Theory

Many times, the education and schooling that migrant students encounter is culturally incongruent with their experiences. The schooling received by migrant students reinforces class structures in curriculum, in representation of students in giftedness and special education programs, in types of available resource materials, in fiscal support and, in educator quality.

Socially just educators must be aware of these inequitable structures that schooling perpetuates as a political act (Giroux, 1985; Nieto, 2010). Culturally proficient educators set in motion mechanisms that will close the gap between migrant students and others in terms of academic success. This can be done by integrating and valuing diversity—in other words, by providing a space for migrant students, their families, and the voice of their communities (Freire, 1981; Bourdieu, 1986).

Difference Theory of Caring

Our role as educators is to care for the profession we have chosen and, most importantly, for the students and families with whom we work. Adapting to diversity by promoting a "culture of caring" is critical in our work with migrant students and their families. Schools can adapt to the diverse migrant student community and their families by exploring with the families their cultural definitions of caring (Antrop-Gonzalez & DeJesus, 2006). Adapting to diversity does not mean watering down the curriculum; rather it is to be "critical and caring" (Hogg, 2012).

MINDFULNESS

Now is another opportunity to "think about your thinking." Use the questions that follow to think about what is possible and about how flexible you and your school are. You may want to return to your journal to record your and your colleagues' thinking.

MY INSIDE-OUT LEARNING PROCESS

- What skills do I possess that support adapting to the diversity of my classroom or school? What skills do I want to learn?
- In what ways have I responded, in the past, when confronted with a need to adapt? What were my feelings? In what ways did I respond? Looking back, in what ways would I have liked to respond? What are you learning about yourself?
- Now that I know what I know about adapting to diversity, what learning or action am I willing to engage in?

Facilitating My School's Inside-Out Learning Process about Adapting to Diversity

- Take a moment to think about some of the issues your school is facing in adapting to students from migrant communities. Describe how the Essential Element—Adapting to Diversity—might inform providing for the social and academic needs of migrant students.
- In what ways might the educators in your school or district work together in adapting to the needs of students from migratory families?

Facilitating My School's Inside-Out Learning Process about Adapting to the Diversity of the Communities We Serve

- In what ways has this chapter impacted your thinking about the diversity of your community?
- List two or three indicators of success that would be evident as your school makes progress in meeting the social and academic needs of students from migratory communities.

THE RUBRIC IN ACTION: ADAPTING TO DIVERSITY FOR INCLUSION AND SUPPORT OF MIGRANT EDUCATION STUDENTS, THEIR FAMILIES, AND THEIR COMMUNITIES

Adapting to Diversity is another important aspect of your and your school's *inside-out* professional learning journey. Consider these steps, which are designed to deepen your knowledge of and facility with the rubric presented in chapter 4.

- As we did in the previous three chapters, take a moment and turn back to Table 4.1, "Educators' Rubric for Inclusion and Support of Migrant Education Students, Their Families, and Their Communities."
- Focus on the Essential Element, Adapting to Diversity. Note how the progression of the illustrations is developmental as you read from Cultural Destructiveness to Cultural Proficiency.
- Next, turn your attention to Table 8.1—Essential Element: Adapting to Diversity for Inclusion and Support of Migrant Education Students, Their Families, and Communities.
- Once again, this table focuses only on the "positive" side of the element.
- The text for Cultural Precompetence, Cultural Competence, and Cultural Proficiency are intended to provide illustrations for individual and organizational use as you plan changes in curriculum, instruction, engagement, and assessment keeping in mind the needs of students from migrant communities.

ESPERANZA COUNTY AND PRÓXIMA ESTACIÓN SCHOOL DISTRICT CASE STORY

This vignette depicts how personnel at the school district and county office are analyzing their understanding of PF students and their families. Administrators, teachers, parents, and staff discuss how to move from personnel-center practices to migrant-oriented programs. The latter provide the space to migrant students and families to explore, explain, and teach personnel about who they are, their needs, and their uniqueness. The former perpetuates a banking model in which personnel work *to* meet migrant students' needs rather than working *with* migrant students and their families to cooperatively enhance current practices with the uniqueness and richness migrant students and their families carry with them as they move from city to city and from the fields to the classroom.

As a Spanish proverb says, "a donde fueres haz lo que vieres" [when being a migrant, learn as migrants do]—in other words, teachers, administrators, and staff must learn first from migrants to better adapt, modify, and tailor their practices to suit the latter's needs.

Participants:

Mr. Tamarit—Migrant Education Program Coordinator
Ms. Castillo—PAC Member
Mr. Zambrano—PAC member
Ms. Rojas—RAC member
Ms. Ponce—SPAC representative
Dr. Reed—Principal, Camino Elementary School

Table 8.1 Essential Element: Adapting to Diversity for Inclusion and Support of Migrant Education Students, Their Families, and Their Communities

Essential Element for Including and Supporting Migrant Students and their Families	Informed by Guiding Principles of Cultural Proficiency		
	Cultural Precompetence	Cultural Competence at Standard	Cultural Proficiency
Adapting to Diversity— Extent to which cultural knowledge is embedded into a moral understanding that leads educator values and school policies to achieve equitable educational and socially just outcomes.	Nurture an authentic personal and school-wide sense of responsibility for learning about each and every migrant culture and language(s) spoken by the migrant community. Study and learn about Regional Applications, District Service Agreements, and Comprehensive Needs Assessments. Demonstrates knowledge in order to disaggregate the academic achievement data and to work with colleagues to interpret and plan for effective use of the data in ways that ensure student academic and personal/social success for all linguistically and culturally diverse migrant students. Build on an initial awareness on the positive reasons of having Regional Applications, District Service Agreements, and Comprehensive Needs Assessments and Family Biliteracy/School Readiness Programs on the importance of disaggregating, analyzing and examining access and opportunity data that explores for disparities among linguistically and culturally diverse migrant students in special education, advanced placement classes, extracurricular activities, and student discipline.	Function as teams to effectively use Regional Applications, District Service Agreements, and Comprehensive Needs Assessments and Family Biliteracy and School Readiness Programs as well as achievement and access/ opportunity data and culturally relevant instructional and curricular content standards to facilitate classroom discussions that represent the cultural and linguistic diversity of migrant students in an inclusive democratic environment. Expound migrant students' ability to access College and Career Readiness and knowledge, and to meet the same challenging academic content standards, make decisions, solve problems, and develop dispositions that will benefit them in an interactive intercultural society.	Using Individual Learning Plans (ILPs) as benchmarks. Systematize school, district and migrant Parent Advisory Councils and parent/guardian groups to examine, analyze and understand opportunity/ access and academic achievement data in a way that considers divergent and often conflicting points of view and leads to equitable and just policies and practices. Confront restrictive legal mandates and catalyze effective efforts intended to meet the needs of all students, with particular attention to Out-of-School Youth and Priority for Service Migrant Students who are linguistically and culturally diverse.

Ms. Sol—Principal, Greenfield Middle School
Mr. Soto—Principal, Adelante High School
Mrs. Del Rio—Counselor, Adelante High School
Ms. Gutierrez—High School Teacher
Mr. Rose—Elementary School Teacher

Mr. Tamarit—Migrant Education Program Coordinator:
*Thank you all for taking the time to attend this meeting. Today, we would like
to extend the dialogue initiated in the last two meetings. For those who did not
participate in those meetings, I would like to summarize what was discussed and
how it is aligned with the focus of today's meeting.*

*As you all know, the Board at the County Office of Education has identified
services and programs for PF students as the main target in our migrant education programs. We have begun to examine our programs and services and
how or if these meet the needs of PF students and their families. In our last
meeting, we shared our understandings on migrant students and their families.
We explored our awareness and its specificity when working with PF students.
Our goal today is to enhance both our understandings and awareness by first
listening to members of PAC, RAC, and SPAC and then formulate how our
programs can not only echo their needs but also to ensure that such programs
are tailored and enriched by the knowledge(s), the culture(s), and language(s)
of migrant students.*

*With no further adieu, let me introduce, Ms. Ponce, who represents Esper-
anza County at the State Parent Advisory Council. Ms. Ponce, the room is yours.*

Ms. Ponce—SPAC representative:
*Gracias [thank you] Ms. Stone. This is a unique opportunity for us to meet
with administrators, teachers, and staff to share a bit about who we are, the
challenges we face, and most importantly to tell you what we would like to see
happening in the migrant program. We have different groups within the migrant
population at Esperanza County. I am not going to bore you with the demographics but we migrants represent different cultures and different languages.
We are thankful for all the services and programs being implemented in our
county. Yet, we feel that we are always being pushed to assimilate within a
system that does not represent who we are. We work hard in the fields. Our children study hard at their schools but we are constantly being asked to change.
We feel that in order to succeed in this system, we have to stop being what we
are and push to becoming who you want us to be.*

Dr. Reed—Principal, Camino Elementary School:
*With all my respect Ms. Ponce, what you are describing is the price all immi-
grants pay when moving to a new place. We cannot expect the place to change.
The ones arriving are the ones who have to adapt and understand how the community works and functions.*

Ms. Rojas—RAC member:

I somehow agree with you. There is no question on the fact we have to adapt if we want to succeed, however what we are saying here is that the school district also needs to learn from who we are. We bring our culture and our language. I always hear, "we are diverse, we are multicultural" and wonder what is the meaning of we? Are we part of this we? Who is to change and learn from?

Mr. Rose—Elementary School Teacher:

Ms. Rojas, I know you and your family. I truly believe that we teachers try our best to understand who you are and modify and adapt our programs to better meet your needs. I am a bit confused by all your questions. Are you implying that we are close-minded, that we do not want to change?

Ms. Rojas—RAC member:

You know Mr. Rose; I respect you and all the teachers. All I am saying is that we do not feel the programs capture who we are, moreover we do not feel part of this multicultural and diverse we.

Ms. Castillo—PAC Member:

What we are saying is that the activities and projects our children complete never analyze and discuss who we are, the problems we are facing, the challenges we overcome. We are part of a we that has forgotten all the Is within. I am Mixteco and I do not remember seeing an activity where my child had the opportunity to think about our culture. May I ask you, Dr. Reed and Mr. Rose, a couple of questions? What do you know about the Mixteco Culture? I am Mixteco and Mr. Zambrano is Zapoteco. Do schools know the differences and similarities of these two millennial cultures?

Ms. Sol—Principal, Greenfield Middle School:

If I can interject, honestly, I do not know too much about these two cultures. I have to admit that oftentimes I label migrant students under one culture, the Mexican culture. I should know better but I do not know.

Mr. Soto, Principal—Adelante High School:

Do not be too hard on yourself, Ms. Sol; we know who the migrant students are. Maybe we do not know about their cultures but we know how to serve them. We have been serving migrant students and their families for decades; did we fail in our tasks because we did not know how to speak Mixteco, because we did not know about their culture? I do not think so.

Ms. Sol—Principal, Greenfield Middle School:

I am not saying that Mr. Soto. I am just saying that I should have known more about them if I want to increase the effectiveness of our programs. How can

*we teach them if we do not really know who they are? How can we teach them
without first learning from them?*

Mrs. Del Rio—Counselor, Adelante High School:
*It takes time to know the students. We are always busy with paperwork, helping
students. I understand the importance of knowing our students but I work with
more than 600 migrant students. Do I know them? No. Would I like to know
more about them? Yes. How could I make this happen? Do I stop working and
scheduling meetings by groups representing different cultures?*

Ms. Gutierrez—High School Teacher:
*That is a good idea. Maybe we can create some units around the different
languages and cultures represented by migrant students. Can we change the
curriculum Mr. Soto?*

Mr. Soto—Principal, Adelante High School:
*We could but we need to involve all the departments. This must be an inter-
departmental effort. Migrant students are taking all the subjects. We can pilot
something at the after-school program or at the Saturday School. The data we
gather can guide us for our summer school programs.*

Mr. Tamarit—Migrant Education Program Coordinator:
*It seems that we are starting a new path. Thank you all for this dialogue. As
Pedro Noguera would say our work is more than just technical work. Our work
is about adapting, we must constantly reflect on who our students are and their
needs. For our meeting, the questions we wanted to answer are as follows: who
are our PF students? What are the needs of our PF students?*

OPPORTUNITY TO JOURNAL

As you think about this new conversation among Próxima Estación educators, reflect on the conversation and respond to the following questions that
resonate for you. Use your journal to record your thinking and questions
that are surfacing for you.

Which participants demonstrated "adapting" behavior? Who? What
evidence do you have? In the conversation among the participants, what
were some of the statements said that made you think there was a need
for changing and adapting practices? Based on this conversation where
might you locate each participant at each of the six points of the Cultural
Proficiency Continuum? Provide evidence for your placements. What are
the next steps you recommend to follow Mr. Tamarit's last statement and
questions?

PROFESSIONAL COMMUNITY LEARNING (PCLs) FOR EDUCATORS WHO TEACH MIGRANT STUDENTS

As the years transcend, communities change, what is less transcendent is the willingness of educators to change and adapt to diversity as those communities change. As educators, being aware of the communities we serve is a first step. What do you believe on the question of who needs to adapt to meet the needs of the migrant students enrolled in your school?

The education of migrant students cannot be left only to the personnel employed by the county or district migrant education programs or teachers who have students who have been identified as migrant students in their classrooms. The entire school community must work together to garner the necessary resources and to set goals in order for migrant students to achieve higher student performance in district and state standardized scores. Higher academic performance and critical thinking skills may be achieved by migrant students by having teachers become knowledgeable of effective teaching practices that include what Goodwin (2012) refers to as the knowledge domains for teaching and for adapting to diversity. These include:

- *Personal knowledge*—by learning about our migrant students and rethinking the concept of "learning" and beliefs about what defines intelligence or achievement;
- *Contextualizing knowledge* is understanding our migrant students, their in-and-out-of-school experiences, as well as their families;
- *Pedagogical knowledge* refers to culturally relevant academic content and curriculum; it integrates social constructivist theories and methods of teaching that take into consideration the learning styles of migrant students;
- *Sociological knowledge*, which includes integrating cultural relevance of diversity into a curriculum that holds a value for social justice and just teaching practices.
- Strategies that schools and communities can adopt to develop *social knowledge* of migrant students and their families is to institute cooperative learning as well as community cooperative activities that develop democratic group processes to address challenges that may arise from the change in demographics and that use the cultural assets and "funds of knowledge" that are inherent in linguistic and culturally diverse ethnic communities (Quezada, Lindsey, & Lindsey, 2012).

When our communities and we educators adapt to diversity, we are prepared to incorporate the optimal point in the Cultural Proficiency approach through intentionally embracing the final essential element, Institutionalizing Cultural Knowledge, which is described and discussed in chapter 9. The use of the five Essential Elements is the extent to which cultural knowledge is evident in educator conduct and in school socially just policies and practices that address educational inequities and tend to close cultural and academic access, opportunity, and achievement gaps therefore advocating for equitable and social just policies and practices in the use of data to inform school of all migrant student and family needs.

When district, migrant education county offices of education and educators make a commitment to effectively serve the needs of migrant students and their families, the Guiding Principles of Cultural Proficiency inform their professional learning and practice. Educators become more mindful of their own values and behaviors as they work with migrant families. They review their own policies and practices of the district and the schools with different lenses, those that place migrant students and their families at the center. Therefore, adapting to diversity is much more difficult as it consistently changes due to migrant family mobility. The many immigrant groups that are represented in the community requires a commitment to using the Guiding Principles of Cultural Proficiency as the foundation for the construction of assessment tools, planning of innovative curriculum, integrating the latest instructional programs and strategies. Further, providing enough resources such as instructional technology support to make sure our migrant students have an opportunity to succeed is of utmost importance.

GOING DEEPER

By now you know that this section is provided for your personal reflection and to guide dialogue with colleagues. The chapter had three parts—descriptions of adapting to diversity in the context of serving children and youth from migratory families, the Essential Element Adapting to Diversity, and a school-based vignette. Take a few moments to think about the content and the Opportunity to Journal material. Pay particular attention to key learning's for you as well as any assumptions about migrant communities that may have been affirmed or challenged.

Reflection Activity

What will it take for your classroom or school to be a place that has successfully adapted to the learning needs of students from migrant communities?

Dialogic Activity

With colleagues in a learning community, a grade-level team, or a department team, engage in a dialogue to reach a shared understanding of what it would take for your school to have a professional learning program that supports the students of migrant communities and which is focused on students learning at levels higher than ever before? What benchmarks would you set for successful implementation of such professional learning programs?

Chapter 9

Institutionalizing Cultural Knowledge—For You, Your School, and the Migrant Communities You Serve

What do you mean by "full responsibility"? If the common good is a matter of decisions we have to make, precisely in the field of political struggle and ecological crisis, is this a term that embraces responsibility even for social reform or revolution?

—ŽiŽek (2014, p. 4)

GETTING CENTERED

By reading to this point in the book, you have covered the Four Tools of Cultural Proficiency that have been presented in depth. This chapter, in combination with chapters 5–8, provides rich descriptions, discussions, and opportunities for personal reflection and dialogue with colleagues. The emphasis in this chapter is on how you, your colleagues, and your school or district should go about learning about the migrant communities represented in your student body.

OPPORTUNITY TO JOURNAL

Take a few moments and ask what questions would you pose to members of the migrant community if you were seeking responses that would give you greater insight about your students? What questions do you ask of yourself, your grade or department level, and about your school or district that would help guide and inform future professional learning?

INSTITUTIONALIZING CULTURAL
KNOWLEDGE FOR ME, MY SCHOOL, AND MY
COMMUNITY AS WE MOVE FORWARD

The fifth and final Essential Element of cultural competence is Institutional-izing Cultural Knowledge. Institutionalizing Cultural Knowledge is accom-plished by utilizing the expertise of migrant and nonmigrant community members as well as educators (funds of knowledge) and sharing their aca-demic and social resource knowledge with others who work with migrant students and their families. Intentionally sharing expertise provides opportu-nity for an increase of opportunities for migrant students and their families to access school and community resources.

As an educator committed to institutionalizing cultural knowledge, you purposefully seek feedback from linguistic and culturally diverse migrant communities, as well as from those communities whose voices and perspec-tives are not heard or listened to and, thereby, fail to address issues of access and academic achievement that affect their children. You assess policies and practices to ensure that equitable and just decisions take into consideration community members' input from the diverse groups across the community, with particular focus on linguistically and culturally diverse migrant students.

This chapter guides you to institutionalize learning as a continuous journey in knowing about your culture and in becoming aware of how your culture is experienced by others. It is through your engagement in personal reflec-tion and dialogue with your colleagues, you are prepared to learn about the culture of your school, the cultures represented among faculty and staff, and the diverse migrant cultures within the community you serve.

INSTITUTIONALIZING CULTURAL KNOWLEDGE
AS A PROFESSIONAL COMMUNITY LEARNING

Institutionalizing cultural knowledge involves use of the *Key School Func-tions* summarized in Table 3.1 aligned with the Essential Elements of Cultural Competence. In using these five Essential Elements of Cultural Competence standards to guide our practices, we shift our learning com-munity language from *professional learning communities* to *professional communities learning*.

Within this framework it becomes a "we" learning approach versus a "they" learning approach; in other words, we as a community take the responsibility to plan and initiate staff development programs that would best support edu-cators working with migrant students and their families in order for them to be sustainable as systemic. We as *Professional Communities Learning* learn together by not utilizing the banking model of professional development, in which we would be the experts and instruction would be a one-way method from "us" to "them."

INSTITUTIONALIZING CULTURAL KNOWLEDGE WITHIN THE MIGRANT EDUCATION PROGRAM CONTEXT

Within the Migrant Education program context, institutionalizing cultural knowledge is the extent to which cultural knowledge is evident in educator conduct and in school policies and practices that address educational inequities and tend to close cultural and academic access, opportunity, and achievement gaps. As an educator, you advocate for equitable and social just policies and practices in the use of data to inform school of all migrant student and family needs.

Using Individual Learning Plans as benchmarks you further advocate for socially just and equitable policies and practices derived from the use of College to Career Readiness information and academic data to inform the school of migrant student needs, with particular emphasis on Out of School Youth and Priority for Service Migrant Students who are linguistically and culturally diverse.

You coach colleagues and community members to develop and use Regional Applications, District Service Agreements, and Comprehensive Needs Assessments and Family Biliteracy and School Readiness Programs to inform themselves about culturally proficient communication strategies to facilitate an understanding among the larger community that meeting the needs of linguistically and culturally diverse migrant students contributes to and supports the education of all students.

You integrate the Innovative Educational Technologies system nationally in order to increase the academic achievement of migrant students. You provide support systems and academic opportunities so that all secondary migrant students meet the academic standards to graduate with a high school diploma (or complete a GED) that prepares them to be College and Career Ready to be admitted to an institution of higher education so they may be responsible and productive citizens, and increase their employment opportunities. You also institutionalize an array of migrant education programs to support elementary, secondary and college migrant students after funding (in some instances) has been depleted or no longer available such as the College Assistance Migrant program, High School Equivalence Program, and California Mini-Corps Program.

TRANSFORMATIVE LEARNING THEORY
AND CRITICAL REFLECTION AS A WAY TO
INSTITUTIONALIZING CULTURAL KNOWLEDGE
IN OUR ACTIONS AND IN OUR PRACTICE

Reflection and dialogue are necessary tools that educators can engage in order to achieve a high level of culturally proficient practices. Reflection in and on our own practice is a foundational tool to transforming and changing our perspectives, as appropriate and necessary, in meeting the needs of students (Mezirow, 1991). In order for educators to institutionalize cultural knowledge to be effective with linguistically and culturally diverse migrant students, we must be engaged in critically reflective dialogue and discourse as part of a Professional Community Learning.

In education, the migrant students' life experiences and their families provide a starting point for transformation. The latter combines life experiences and critical reflection on how migrant students are able to make shifts in their world-views. According to Mezirow (1997b), "We transform our frames of references through critical reflection on the assumptions upon which our interpretations, beliefs, and habits of mind or points of view are based" (p. 7). This process of self-reflection is key to significant personal transformations to becoming culturally proficient as educators and institutionalizing key policies and practices when we work with our migrant students and their families.

This disconnect experienced by migrant students in schools means their existing knowledge is not enough to make sense of the contradictions one is experiencing in schools. According to Kiely (2005), "effects of high-intensity dissonance do not go away, they create permanent markers in students' frame of reference" (p. 11). Many times this dissonance causes migrant students to lose interest in school and fail in their academics, which in turn causes them to drop out of school. This points to the potential of experiential learning for creating the highly dissonant conditions under which transformative learning occurs (Cunningham & Grossman, 2009).

Critical Reflection

The concept of reflection has been used for decades as an aspect of learning and education. Reflection is the "active, persistent, and careful consideration of any belief or supposed form of knowledge in the light of the grounds to support it and further conclusions to which it tends" (Dewey, 1933, p. 9). Reflection in the context of learning is a generic term for those intellectual and affective activities where individuals engage themselves in order to explore their experiences so it may lead to new understandings and appreciations (Boud & Walker, 1985, p. 19). Reflective thinking can lead to expansion of the range or intensity of a point of view by introducing new perspectives, addressing misconceptions, confronting biases, or challenging assumptions. Reflective thinking can also lead to shifts in *habits of mind.*

Education for Transformative Learning

Transformative learning involves experiencing a deep, structural shift in the basic premises of thought, feelings, and actions of people and their organizations (O'Sullivan, 2003).

> Such a shift involves our understanding of ourselves and our self-locations; our relationships with others and with the natural world; our understanding of relations of power in structures of class, race and gender; our body awareness, our visions of alternative approaches to living; and our sense of possibilities for social justice and peace and personal job. (O'Sullivan, 2003, p. x)

Transformative learning requires a form of education in which critical reflection and awareness of frame of reference are key elements in setting educational objectives and in evaluating learner growth (Mezirow, 1997b).

Integrating transformative learning theory into professional communities' learning plans can assist in institutionalizing cultural knowledge to better serve migrant students, as the learning plans must be long term and collaborative, and include continuous learning for educators to grow and develop our knowledge of the cultural and linguistically diverse migratory communities we serve. In addition, the professional communities learning plan will provide professional resources for migrant families to address access and achievement for their children. By engaging in critical reflection, dialogue, and discourse, we can move forward in institutionalizing cultural knowledge that enables school personnel to make equitable and socially just decisions for the betterment of migrant students and their families.

Schools that have been successful with culturally and linguistically diverse students engage in processes of self-reflection to assess their practices and critically reflect on their ideologies, perspectives, beliefs, and attitudes that lead to necessary changes in instruction when working with migrant students (Quezada, Lindsey, & Lindsey, 2012). Educators begin to shift their attitudes and beliefs away from effective schools and communities being a one-size-fits-all solution. Culturally proficient educators consider Herrera and Murray's (2005) teaching practices in order to meet the needs of migrant students and their families through an instructional and ideological mind shift created when these 10 steps are taken:

- Acknowledging that linguistically and culturally diverse migrant students have not done well academically and socially in our classrooms and across the district, even with the support of the migrant education program.
- Identifying similarities and differences in teaching linguistically and culturally diverse migrant students with effective practices based on research that is specifically conducted to address the needs of migrant students and their families.
- Challenging one's beliefs about one's own teaching practice when compared to theory, and research-based practices specifically tailored for teaching migrant students.
- Recognizing that educators teaching migrant students face the same challenges in teaching practices when teaching other culturally and linguistically diverse student populations.
- Researching and gathering information on best culturally relevant theories and teaching practices from peers and others that specifically address the needs of migrant students and their families.
- Understanding why certain instructional methods and programs are more effective with particular linguistically and culturally diverse migrant students.
- Creating and implementing Professional Community Learning plans for utilizing newly adopted methods that specifically target migrant students.
- Experimenting with and adapting new instructional methods that will support the education of migrant students so they may achieve academic success.

MINDFULNESS—OPPORTUNITY TO JOURNAL

With this fifth and final Essential Element, you have the opportunity to "think about your thinking." Use the questions that follow to think about what is possible and about the flexibility that you see within yourself and your school. You may want to return to your journal to record your thinking as well as that of your colleagues.

My Inside-Out Learning Process:

- In what ways does this Essential Element, Institutionalizing Cultural Knowledge, support the four preceding Essential Elements?
- In what way can I make these Essential Elements part of my personal and professional practice?
- Now that I know what I know about Institutionalizing Cultural Knowledge, to what learning or action am I willing to commit?

- Implementing selected methods that support instruction of migrant students based on research as a foundation of professional development and practice.
- Evaluate educational learning outcomes during and after the implementation of teaching practices that support migrant students based on professional feedback (Herrera & Murray, p. 339).

These practices can be the impetus to proceed from valuing migrant students and their families as possessing unique cultural assets to Institutionalizing Cultural Knowledge in ways that provides effective, socially just, and equitable migrant education services. In professional environments where educators institutionalize the acquisition of cultural knowledge migrant students are much more likely to experience academic and social success.

Facilitating My School's Inside-Out Learning Process about Institutionalizing Cultural Knowledge

- What might be issues facing our school while serving students from migrant communities that might be alleviated by taking on board the Essential Element, Institutionalizing Cultural Knowledge?
- To what degree are we aware of policies and practices that impact the programs for our students from migratory families?
- In what ways might educators and parents work together to institutionalize culturally proficient practices to meet the social and academic needs of our students from migratory families?

Facilitating My School's Inside-Out Learning Process for Institutionalizing Cultural Knowledge About the Communities We Serve

- In what ways might this chapter inform my work with the wider community our school serves?
- How might I incorporate this chapter's message with our plan to better serve students from migratory families?
- In what ways might we serve and partner with our communities to *institutionalize our cultural knowledge* in support of all learners?
- What might be some indicators that will help us determine if our students from migratory families are benefiting from our school's use of culturally proficient practices?

THE RUBRIC IN ACTION: INSTITUTIONALIZING CULTURAL KNOWLEDGE FOR INCLUSION AND SUPPORT OF MIGRANT EDUCATION STUDENTS, THEIR FAMILIES, AND THEIR COMMUNITIES

Institutionalizing Cultural Knowledge is the final, integral component of the "inside-out" learning process for you, your school, and your school's relationship with your school's diverse community, once again with particular emphasis on students from migratory families. When, Institutionalizing Cultural Knowledge is embraced as a standard of individual behavior or school policy educators and their schools begin to be intentional with their behaviors, in their policies, and practices that effectively serve students from migratory families and communities. Consider these steps as you continue to analyze the rubric presented in chapter 4.

Take a moment and refer back to chapter 4, Table 4.1, "Educators' Rubric for Inclusion and Support of Migrant Education Students, Their Families, and Their Communities."

- As before, you will note, when reading from left to right across the row of the rubric, Institutionalizing Cultural Knowledge, the developmental nature of moving from Cultural Destructiveness to Cultural Proficiency.
- Now turn your attention to Table 9.1 that presents Institutionalizing Cultural Knowledge of the rubric from chapter 4. By now, it easy for you to note that:
  - Table 9.1 includes only the "positive" side of the rubric. Of course, in your role as an educator you will hear comments and become aware of practices represented on the left side of the continuum. The rubric is designed for the right side to provide Culturally Precompetent, Competent, and Proficient choices when responding to individual comments and school practices located on the left side, which is represented as Cultural Destructiveness, Incapacity, or Blindness.

    Effective use of the rubric depends, in large part, on awareness of yours and others' unhealthy comments or practices and, then, consulting the right side of the rubric for healthy comments or practices to be used by you and your colleagues. It is the process of recognizing and acknowledging placement of comments or practices on the rubric that deepens the inside-out process of change for you and your school. Likewise, it is the inside-out processes inherent in personal reflection and collegial dialogue that provides opportunity for you and the school to grow as a Professional Community Learning.
  - When reading the illustrations for Cultural Precompetence, Competence, and Proficiency in Table 9.1, pay particular attention to adjectives and

Table 9.1 Essential Element: Institutionalizing Cultural Knowledge for Inclusion and Support of Migrant Education Students, Their Families, and Their Communities

Essential Elements for Including and Supporting Migrant Students and Their Families	Informed by Guiding Principles of Cultural Proficiency		
	Cultural Precompetence	*Cultural Competence at Standard*	*Cultural Proficiency*
Institutionalizing Cultural Knowledge—Extent to which cultural knowledge is evident in educator conduct and in school socially just policies and practices that address educational inequities and tend to close cultural and academic access, opportunity, and achievement gaps. Advocates for equitable and social just policies and practices in the use of data to inform school of all migrant student and family needs.	Recognize through data analyses that Family Biliteracy and School Readiness Programs achievement gaps are persistent and begin to pay attention to inequities inherent in student access and opportunity that leads to inappropriate academic placement. Start to question the unequal distribution of available and appropriate human, educational, health and financial resources that supports professional development for appropriately serving linguistically and culturally diverse migrant students.	Promote and support Regional Applications, District Service Agreements, and Comprehensive Needs Assessments and Family Biliteracy and School Readiness Programs in order to sponsor opportunities for sharing expertise among school personnel to address access and College and Career Readiness opportunities for linguistically and culturally diverse migrant students and families. Deliberately seek input from linguistically and culturally diverse communities, inclusive of those who do not assert their voices or perspectives, to address access and achievement issues for their children.	Using ILP as benchmarks advocate for socially just and equitable policies and practices derived from the use of College to Career Readiness and academic data to inform school of migrant student needs, with particular emphasis on Out-of-School Youth and Priority for Service Migrant Students who are linguistically and culturally diverse.

(Continued)

Table 9.1   Essential Element: Institutionalizing Cultural Knowledge for Inclusion and Support of Migrant Education Students, Their Families, and Their Communities

Essential Elements for Including and Supporting Migrant Students and Their Families	Informed by Guiding Principles of Cultural Proficiency		
	Cultural Precompetence	Cultural Competence at Standard	Cultural Proficiency
	Risk being overwhelmed by the size of closing academic achievement gaps for migrant students and decide to do little or nothing, and revert to counterproductive practices and policies. Actively utilize the Migrant Student Information Network and Migrant Student Record Exchange system. To inform the school district, county, region and state on how to allow migrant students an opportunity to accrue loss of school credits due to their or their families' agricultural migrant mobility.	Measure Regional Applications, District Service Agreements, and Comprehensive Needs Assessments and Family Biliteracy and School Readiness Programs to align policies and practices to make equitable decisions that consider all community members' input, with particular focus on linguistically and culturally diverse migrant students. Apply an evidence-based Regional Applications, District Service Agreements, and Comprehensive Needs Assessments and Family Biliteracy and School Readiness Programs to support College to Career Readiness educational programs and consistently follow student placement decisions established on multiple academic and cultural measures that include language proficiency (i.e., English and home).	Pursue to use College to Career Readiness and academic data to inform school progress in narrowing and closing academic achievement gaps of Out-of-School Youth and Priority for Service Migrant Students who are linguistically and culturally diverse. Coach colleagues and community members to develop and use Regional Applications, District Service Agreements, and Comprehensive Needs Assessments and Family Biliteracy and School Readiness Programs to inform them about culturally proficient communication strategies to facilitate an understanding among the larger community that meeting the needs of linguistically and culturally diverse migrant students contributes to and supports the education of all students.

Ensure that all secondary migrant students reach challenging academic standards and graduate with a high school diploma (or complete a GED) that prepares them for responsible citizenship, further learning, and productive employment.

Apply and seeks funding for an array of innovative and additional Migrant Education Initiatives to support the academic achievement of elementary, secondary and college migrant students (i.e., College Assistance Migrant program (CAMP), High School Equivalence Program (HEP), Migrant Mini-Corps) as well as Teacher Regional and State Student and Parents Leadership Programs and Institutes.

Develop national leadership initiatives to increase the capacity of State educational agencies, local school districts, schools, and other community organizations to continuously improve the educational outcomes attained by migrant students.

Integrate the Innovative Educational Technologies system nationally in order to increase the academic achievement of migrant students.

Provides support systems and academic opportunities so that all secondary migrant students meet the academic standards to graduate with a high school diploma (or complete a GED) that prepares them to be College and Career Ready to be admitted to an institution of higher education so they may responsible and productive citizens, and increase their employment opportunities.

Institutionalizes an array of migrant education programs to support elementary, secondary and college migrant students after funding (in some instances) has been depleted or no longer available such as College Assistance Migrant program (CAMP), High School Equivalence Program (HEP), Migrant Mini-Corps.

Source: Adapted from Reyes L. Quezada, Delores B. Lindsey, & Randall B. Lindsey.(2012). *Cultural Proficiency Practice-Educators Supporting English Learning Students,* Thousand Oaks, CA: Corwin.

verbs and note both the active voice and intentionality. The inside-out process for individuals and organizations is about being intentional, or mindful in creating values, beliefs, and behaviors that belie personal and organizational change.

Institutionalizing cultural knowledge of your school, the school district, your migrant program and community represents the phase in the cultural proficiency journey where the change process in your beliefs and values regarding working with migrant students and families is manifested. In this phase, it is evident that as you confront and overcome the resistance to change where you know individuals who continue to perpetuate the "that" it is the migrant students and their families "that" are the ones who need to conform and adapt to current school practices. You now realize and understand that it is "we," as educators, also who have responsibility to grow and learn in meeting the needs of our diverse, asset-rich migrant populations.

As in previous chapters, and in order to attain socially just and equitable schools and programs for migrant students, we invite you to revisit the discussion in chapter 2 about how the Guiding Principles of Cultural Proficiency serve as a moral and ethical framework of Cultural Proficiency, thereby informing the healthy right side of the rubric. You will see in the vignette that follows, Dr. Goldman approaches the inside-out approach to change by modeling an appropriate view for the school district. He provides the vision of how Esperanza County is building a systematic, strategic approach when working with migrant students and their families.

With the focus on the PF students, the leadership team analyzes the analysis of practices conducted at Próxima Estación School District and how the outcomes of this process could serve to inform other school districts seeking to institutionalize cultural knowledge. The leadership team is designing well-defined goals as the key to build accountability structures that ensure successful implementation of culturally and linguistically responsive practices. Moreover, the team is committed to work cooperatively with all the parties—parents, students, teachers, and staff—involved in this transformative initiative. Take a few moments to read the vignette and discern the evidence of progression throughout the cultural proficiency framework and how it is represented in educators' moral and ethical actions throughout their discussion.

ESPERANZA COUNTY AND PRÓXIMA ESTACIÓN SCHOOL DISTRICT

Esperanza County's assistant superintendent is meeting with the leadership team.

Dr. Goldman—Esperanza County, Superintendent:

I want to thank you for joining us today as we continue the series of meetings to analyze our practices when working with PF migrant students. As you all know, the County Board has identified this area as a priority for the Migrant Education Program and all the school districts serving migrant students. The County Board carefully read and discussed the Comprehensive Needs Assessment conducted by an external evaluation team and determined the necessity of designing a plan and tools to analyze practices and programs implemented with migrant students and their families.

Moreover, the County Board recommended that we select one school district to pilot such examination to later share the outcomes of this study with all the schools districts serving migrant students and their families. In today's meeting, we will present the evaluation conducted at Próxima Estación School District. The goal is to reflect on your practices and to transform and enhance our programs as we meet the needs of Pf students and their families. Thank you all for being here today and for your willingness to explore new paths and programs in Migrant Education. Dr. Ceballos the floor is yours. Gracias.

Dr. Ceballos—Esperanza County, Assistant Superintendent:

Thank you Dr. Goldman for your leadership in this process. As Dr. Goldman has explained, we are revising our practices and programs in Migrant Education. Following the recommendations highlighted at the Comprehensive Needs Assessment, our programs could better meet the needs of our migrant students, specifically our PF students, if we are more strategic and conscious when examining the programs we are currently implementing and how these are aligned to the needs and distinct traits of our PF students. It seems that our programs are somehow disconnected with the needs of PF students.

Moreover, we have to reflect if our programs are designed and tailored to effectively serve migrant students or we are just implementing programs without recognizing the uniqueness and richness migrant students and their families bring to our schools. With that, I will ask Mr. Perez the process followed at Próxima Estación School District and how this could inform similar processes to be conducted in your school districts.

Mr. Perez—Migrant Education Regional Director:

Thank you Dr. Ceballos. We the Migrant Education Office truly believe that the synergy between the county office and school districts is key to maximizing the programs and services we offer to migrant students and their families. The findings of the Comprehensive Needs Assessment taught us that we have some areas in which we can refine our programs. Moreover, we learned that in order to increase the effectiveness of our programs, we have to develop systematic and strategic approaches. We must support teachers and staff who are working with migrant students. The support begins by rethinking, self-evaluating, and dialoguing on our understandings of where our migrant students are, the funds of knowledge they posses and the specific challenges they face when navigating

*the educational system. Change, if to occur, calls for an all-inclusive transfor-
mation of our practices.*

*To better understand what processes are needed to institutionalize additive
attitudes and practices when working with migrant students, we asked Mr. Zarzoso and his team to conduct a series of research meetings on the limitations,
needs, and constrains of their migrant programs. Mr. Zarzoso, could you please
outline the key elements of this process at your school district?*

Mr. Zarzoso—Superintendent at Próxima Estación School District (PESD):
*Thank you Mr. Perez. Let me start by concurring on your description of positive
synergy across educational agencies. We at PESD promote and look for partnerships and collaborations to enhance our services to our students and their
families. If I have to be honest, our migrant programs had fallen into a cycle of
implementation without revision. We implemented programs but we barely took
time to reflect on the data, if any, generated by these programs. I am taking
ownership on the lack of reflective practices.*

*We needed to be proactive and mindful but instead we were complacent and
somehow disconnected from what was needed and requested by migrant families. The examination of our programs has helped us tremendously to see the
areas in which we need to work moving forward.*

*Before I pass the turn to Ms. Stone, I would like to thank the County Office for
its support and guidance in this process. We never felt judged, to the contrary,
we encountered this opportunity as a venue to rethink not only our practices,
as organization, with migrant students but as a prospect to redefine who PESD
is now and how we want to look in the years to come. Thank you once again.
Ms. Stone, the floor is yours.*

**Ms. Stone—Assistant Superintendent for Educational Instruction
at Próxima Estación School District:**
*Thank you Mr. Zarzoso. I would like to outline the findings of our analysis.
During our conversations and analysis of previous DSAs, we found that we
needed:*

- *A better alignment between programs and the needs described on student's
  ILPs*
- *To develop a new ILP that will capture both quantitative and qualitative data*
- *Training on understanding the cultural richness of the different migrant groups*
- *Design evaluation tools to inform and assess our practices*
- *Use data to adapt, modify, and/or eliminate programs*
- *Include all the parties—parents, teachers, and staff—in programmatic decisions*
- *Better understand the needs of our PF students*

*There are other areas included in these themes, but the ones I just shared with
you are the framework for our action plan, which, if possible, could be aligned
with your action plans; thus, we develop a cohesive implementation.*

Dr. Cisneros—Superintendent at Goose Creek School District:
I am just wondering how your analysis and action plan can be aligned with our hypothetic action plan. How do you know we have the same needs? Do you have any evidence that our DSAs require the same improvement? I think our migrant students are well served with the programs we are currently implementing.

Dr. Ceballos—Esperanza County, Assistant Superintendent:
If I may interject Dr. Cisneros, what Ms. Stone just shared typifies the findings of the CNA we conducted for the whole program. There were some differences across school districts, but overall the DSAs showed similar strengths and parallel areas of improvement. The final goal is to enhance our practices, which will require that we work together as a team.

Mr. Cienfuegos—Superintendent at Montaña Bonita School District:
What you are saying Dr. Ceballos is that we need to go through the same process PEDS completed before we build our action plan together. What kind of support did the county provide to PEDS? Was it with money, personnel, guidelines?

Dr. Casemiro—Superintendent at Hidden Hill School District:
I thought about the same questions. You are asking us to spend more time analyzing our practices because it seems our practices lack in effectiveness and are disconnected from the reality migrant students and their families face in daily basis.

Dr. Ceballos—Esperanza County, Assistant Superintendent:
You are absolutely right. The reality is that we need to review our practices. We must train our personnel to understand the uniqueness and richness of our migrant students and their families. For years, we have served our migrant students with programs designed for other populations—i.e., ELs, Immigrant.

Though many of our students fall under these categories, they have an important trait that is missing in our programs: the use of their knowledge and their experiences to contextualize and frame our practices. It seems, as we, with all the respect, are blind to who are migrant students are: either we group them based on past practices or we are satisfied with isolated stories of success. We want success for all, we want to serve them all with the best high quality programs. We need equity now. Equality is not meeting their needs, rather it generalizes and hides our weaknesses.

Mrs. Ferrer—Superintendent at Gavina School District:
Wow, strong message and ideas. The whole dialogue somehow surprises me. It sounds like we have left our migrant students behind. How did this happen? Why are we being so conscious now? Where was the accountability and support before?

Dr. Goldman—Esperanza County, Superintendent:

I would like for everyone to be reflective rather than to feel like we have failed an exam. We have done outstanding things in the migrant education program. Your leadership has been instrumental when serving our migrant students and families. We like any other program have to review our practices. Our migrant students today are different from the ones we served twenty years ago. Therefore we need to evaluate our views, our practices and most importantly our competence. As Parker J. Palmer (2007) states "the deep and abiding real-ity—the reality we do not invent, the reality we have to cope with—is that we are interconnected beings born in and for community" (intro, p. xxix)

Migrant students are an essential part of our community. We can separate them from our reality and keep saying "we are serving them" but the truth is that our county among many other features is a "migrant county." Let's embrace and learn from this reality. Let's make it happen.

OPPORTUNITY TO JOURNAL

Take a moment to locate your journal and after reading the following questions, when ready, capture your responses as well as any new questions that may surface for you.

What are some of the different ideas being discussed by the leadership team in order to understand the concept of institutionalizing cultural knowledge? Based on the current conversation, where might you place the leadership team on each of the rubric's five essential elements? What evidence can you extract from the discussion that supports your assessment? What are the next steps the leadership team must follow to meet the goals they have set? Do you see similar patterns in your school, district, county, or organization?

PROFESSIONAL COMMUNITIES LEARNING TOGETHER IN INSTITUTIONALIZING CULTURAL KNOWLEDGE

Chapter 10 and the Resources section of this book offer professional communities learning activities aligned with each of the Essential Elements. Chapter 10 has a focus on Institutionalizing Cultural Knowledge presented in this chapter and illustrated in the *Esperanza County and Próxima Estación School District* case story. Take a moment and turn to chapter 10 and familiarize yourself with the book study protocol. From our professional experience book study processes provide a supportive environment for bringing to light the effectiveness with migrant students and their families, as well as other learners.

GOING DEEPER

This chapter presented the Essential Element of Institutionalizing Cultural Knowledge. We offered a final vignette from the *Esperanza County and Próxima Estación School District* case story as an illustration a county entity and its school district providing leadership informed by culturally proficient values and practices in the context of changing demographics in terms of the growing number of students from migratory families in county, school districts, and communities.

The chapter presented the rubric in Table 9.1 to assist educators and school teams in institutionalizing policies and practices for working cross-culturally students and families from migratory communities. Reflective questions for you and meditational questions for your learning communities were to guide your thinking about practice. A professional learning strategy was presented to support you, your colleagues, and the community in which you serve institutionalize the cultural knowledge you have gained about the rich diversity within your larger school community and, in particular, your migratory communities.

Now is the opportune time to consider some key learning's that are emerging for you. What assumptions about your students from migratory families were you holding? In what ways have these assumptions guided your teaching behaviors? To what extent were the assumptions helpful or a hindrance to your being successful with students from migratory families? What assumptions do you hold about students' migratory families? In what ways have these assumptions guided your decisions about curriculum, instruction, and assessment? You may want to return to your journal and proceed to the reflection and dialogic activities that follow.

Reflection Activity

Now that you know what you know, and you have surfaced and examined your assumptions, about Institutionalizing Cultural Knowledge, what are you willing to do? What might it take to create a school and community culture in support of students from migratory families and communities?

Dialogic Activity

With a group of your colleagues, enter into dialogue for the purpose of achieving shared understanding of *a professional development program in support of students from migratory families performing at levels higher than ever before.* Continue the dialogue throughout small learning communities in the school, the district, and in your county. Once shared understanding has been reached, proceed to consider what might be some resources, strategies, and structures that could be planned, developed and implemented to support students from migratory families, as well as other learners?

Part III concludes this book by ending with chapter 10 which presents you with a three-day professional model in order for you to take action to better equip educators who work with migrant students and their families! Therefore, now that you have learned about how you and how educators can work toward becoming culturally proficient, what are you willing to do to better serve migrant students and their families?

Part III

NEXT STEPS

Table 3.1 aligns the *Key School Functions* model with the Five Essential Elements of Cultural Competence in ways to inform educators' professional learning for working more intentionally with migrant communities (Lindsey, Jungwirth, Pahl, & Lindsey, 2009). We offer the *Key School Functions* model as a *focus* for you in Part III of this book.

Institutionalizing cultural knowledge entails the extent to which professional learning addresses cultural issues, how it addresses issues of cultural identity, how it promotes and models the use of inquiry and dialogue related to multiple perspectives and issues arising from diversity, how it facilitates change to meet the needs of the community, and how it shapes policies and practices that meet the needs of a diverse community. Therefore, this model addresses and supports your journey in the planning of a holistic Professional Community Learning educator development plan that can meet the needs of educators who work with migrant students and their families so that they may have full access to best practices in the *Four Key Functions* of our schools in curriculum and instruction, assessment, parents and community, and professional development.

Chapter 10

Professional Communities Learning Together to Improve Migrant Students' Academic and Social Outcomes

If I want to teach [and learn from migrant families] well, it is essential that I explore my inner terrain. But I can get lost in there, practicing self-delusion and running in self-serving circles. So I need the guidance that a community of collegial discourse provides.

—Parker J. Palmer (2007, p. 146)

GETTING CENTERED

Take a few moments and reread Parker Palmer's words in the epigraph above. What thoughts come to mind as you read his words? What are your feelings and reactions after reading his words? Now that you have read this far in this book, what questions do you have for your own learning about migrant families served by your school? What questions do you still have that might guide the professional learning for your teachers working with migrant students, your school, your district, or the regional migrant education program?

OPPORTUNITY TO JOURNAL

Mull over the questions raised above and, then, please return to your journal to record your thoughts, feelings or reactions, and questions.

We expect that reading chapters 5–9 would have enabled you to analyze your personal and professional views and educational practices when working with and learning from migrant students and their families. Further, we hope that you would have examined vignettes depicting scenarios of Migrant Education Program personnel having discussions on issues affecting migrant students and their families and asked yourself how these discussions relate to each behavior along the cultural proficiency rubric. We intend for you to use the rubric to guide your actions, as well as those of your school, to align with actions described under "cultural competence" and "cultural proficiency" for each of the five essential elements.

In this chapter, we propose a sequence of professional development activities to channel your thoughts and ideas, as these will build a *collegial discourse*, which will inform key components—District Service Agreements (DSA), Regional Applications (RA), Comprehensive Needs Assessment (CNA), and State Service Delivery Plan (SSDP)—when developing effective and comprehensive programs and services for migrant students and their families.

PROFESSIONAL LEARNING

The goal of professional learning activities is to bridge the reader's self-dialogue, which we refer to as reflection throughout this book, with the dialogic self-examinations of his or her colleagues working with and learning from migrant students and their families. As Palmer (2007) explains, individual ideas and views could be lost without the context and support of proactive collegiality. Following are steps to guide you when designing and implementing professional learning activities. Using the Design Thinking Framework (http://www.designthinkingforeducators.com/design-thinking/), we propose a sequence of activities participants will complete throughout a two- to three-day professional learning workshop. Ideally, participants would have read the entire book prior to attending the workshop. If not, reading activities from various components of the chapters could be selected for use throughout the two- to three-day professional learning workshop.

Reflection

To what are you willing to commit as you think about your commitment to your own professional learning? In thinking about your school or districts, migrant education regional program, ask yourself what assets are in place to support professional learning related to migrant education? What obstacles might impede professional learning on this topic? This is an important step, so use your journal to record your comments. We'll return to these questions later in the chapter.

PROFESSIONAL COMMUNITY LEARNING STRATEGY

Activity 1—Alignment of Migrant Student Individual Learning Plans (ILPs)
The provider of the professional learning workshops in conjunction with the leadership team of migrant education programs in county offices or district offices or both identifies a key topic to be analyzed during the professional learning workshops. For example, workshops could examine, as proposed in the Cultural Proficiency rubric, the essential element Cultural Proficiency, alignment between ILPs and the objectives and expected outcomes of Language Arts and Math Programs designed to increase the student achievement and college readiness of migrant students.

Activity 2—Migrant Program Practices and Professional Community Learning Norms
(a) The provider will present a key topic as this relates to the practices of all migrant education personnel—that is, recruiters, paraprofessionals, teachers, administrators, and parents. If we use the aforesaid example—alignment between ILPs and program objectives and outcomes—the PD provider will introduce the importance to analyze trends or needs across ILPs and how these needs must guide program design. After the key topic is introduced the participants will respond to the following five questions.
(b) Each participant responds to these five questions:
  1. I have a challenge—how do I approach it? How do I approach the alignment between ILP and program design?
  2. I learned something—how do I interpret it? How do I interpret the data included on the ILPs?
  3. I see an opportunity—what do I create? How do I create programs that better meet the needs of migrant students and their families?
  4. I have an idea—how do I build it? How do I align students' needs with the objectives and outcomes of the program?
  5. I have tried something—how do I evolve it? How do I evaluate the implementation of the program in terms of both outputs and outcomes?
(c) Participants will share their responses with their colleagues. As they share their responses it is important to remember five basic rules (Rodríguez-Valls, 2009) of engaging in productive and mindful dialogues:
  1. Actively listen if you want to be heard.
  2. Respect if you want to be appreciated.

3. Share if you want to be fair.
4. Welcome ideas if you want to be invited.
5. Assist if you want to be helped.

Activity 3—Book Study as a Professional Community Learning Strategy
As previously discussed in the introduction of this chapter—migrant and non-migrant personnel could be involved in long-term professional development whereby they meet as a professional community learning together or during the two- to three-day workshop to discuss practices that can support migrant students and their families.

Book Study can be a strong tool to develop expertise and improve performance and enhancing student and staff learning through intentional and deliberate practice. What follows are *Going Deeper* discussion and reaction questions to particular chapters to support the dialogue during the book study. You will have been involved and experienced journaling opportunities throughout this book and, therefore, through *Book Study* you will deepen this experience.

Your journaling can take many forms such as your personal journal, through blogs, or shared with others through drop box and google drive and school networks. Chapter discussions can be led by the facilitator, a group member, or individually on your own. The Professional Community Learning Norms in Activity 2c as described by Rodríguez-Valls (2009) can serve as the framework to a healthy and mindful discussion. Enjoy the journey!

Chapter 2—The Tools of Cultural Proficiency for Educator Use

Going Deeper Discussion Questions to Consider

- From your own perspective, name and describe the Tools of Cultural Proficiency.
- The *Inside-Out Process* is the key to understanding one's cultural proficiency journey, describe how you interpret its meaning?
- Do you believe that reflection and dialogue support the *Inside-Out Process*? If so, why?
- Culture and language are embraced as assets that support Cultural Proficiency. Describe how and why you believe this is so?
- The Guiding Principles are essential core values that support how you view yourself and your school. In what ways are the Guiding Principles consistent with your views?
- The Guiding Principles counter the Barriers to Cultural Proficiency. Explain how you may use them in a discussion to your advantage.

- Describe how the Essential Elements provide you with "action" steps on your journey toward Cultural Proficiency?

Going Deeper Discussion and Reflection Questions to Consider

- What is your personal reaction to the Barriers of the Cultural Proficiency Section and to the Guiding Principles as core values?
  - Describe how each of the Essential Elements are informed and supported by the Guiding Principles.
  - In what manner do the Essential Elements serve as standards for personal, and professional behavior toward achieving Cultural Proficiency?
- What is your reaction, personally or professionally, as you become acquainted with the Tools of Cultural Proficiency?
- What other knowledge is needed by you to learn about Cultural Proficiency to help you in your journey to becoming a culturally proficient educator or individual?

Chapter 5—Assessing Cultural Knowledge—From Self-Centered Learning to Socially Just Student- and Community-Asset Learning

Going Deeper Discussion Questions to Consider

- In what ways do the Essential Elements serve as standards for professional community learning to better support migrant students and their families?
- How might the Essential Elements be useful for you and your school as you work with migrant students and their families?
- In what ways might studying the Comprehensive Needs Assessments data about *PF* migrant student access and achievement inform *Assessing Cultural Knowledge*?
- In what ways do Dr. Ceballos and her colleagues describe the importance of *Assessing Cultural Knowledge of PF migrant students*?

Going Deeper Discussion and Reaction Questions to Consider

- Describe how you believe Cultural Proficiency to be a *journey.*
- What is your understanding of *Assessing Cultural Knowledge*? How would you describe it to a colleague?
- In what ways can you and your school and your migrant education region personnel use the information from this chapter to better understand migrant students and their families?

Chapter 6—Valuing Diversity Is Reflected in the Beliefs and Values You and Your School Hold, and How You Share Those Beliefs and Values with Your Community

Going Deeper Discussion Questions to Consider

- Describe how you believe the Essential Element *Valuing Diversity* informs your learning journey.
- What is your understanding of *Valuing Diversity*? How would you describe it to a colleague?
- Valuing diversity of migrant students and their families is a blind spot in the case story discussion. What is the focus of the conversation? Who needs assistance and why do you think it is needed?

Going Deeper Discussion and Reflection Questions to Consider

- Describe your thoughts and personal beliefs and reactions about this chapter. In what ways do your beliefs and reactions inform the use of educational and community support systems for migrant students and their families?
- In what ways can you and your school, in league with the migrant education region personnel, use the information from this chapter to better understand migrant students and their families?

Chapter 7—Managing the Dynamics of Difference to Make a Difference

Going Deeper Discussion Questions to Consider

- Describe the Essential Element *Managing the Dynamics of Difference— what does it convey?*
- How can you make sure that managing the dynamics of difference help support the cultural assets migrant students and their families bring to schools? In what ways can learning communities be inclusive and vibrant?
- Managing the Dynamics of Difference of migrant students and their families is central to the discussion in the case story—What do you think to be the focal point of the dialogue? How can program services to migrant students be enhanced, based on your experience with migrant students and their families?

Going Deeper Discussion and Reflection Questions to Consider

- What were your thoughts and personal reactions about the information in this chapter? In what ways do your reactions inform your future choices for working with migrant students in your school, the district, or migrant regional county office?

- How has the information from this chapter helped you? In what ways do you believe the information in this chapter to be of value to personnel in district or regional migrant county offices?

Chapter 8—Adapting to Diversity—As a Team in the Schools and Communities We Serve

Going Deeper Discussion Questions to Consider

- What do you believe is conveyed by the Essential Element, *Adapting to Diversity*?
- Equitable Shared Accountability is aligned with *Adapting to Diversity. Why is this important*?
- Adapting to the diversity of migrant students and their families is a part of the discussion in the case story—How would you describe the focus of the dialogue to a colleague who has not read the vignette? In what ways can school personnel learn about and integrate the cultural assets migrant student populations and their families bring to their schools?

Going Deeper Discussion and Reflection Questions to Consider

- Describe your thoughts and personal reactions about the information in this chapter? How have your reactions informed your future choices for working with migrant students in your school, the district, or migrant regional county office?
- How has the information from this chapter helped you in working with your district, regional, or county migrant education office? In what ways can this information be used by you or by your school?

Chapter 9—Institutionalizing Cultural Knowledge—for You, Your School, and the Migrant Communities You Serve

Going Deeper Discussion Questions to Consider

- Describe, what you believe the Essential Element *Institutionalizing Cultural Knowledge* is attempting to convey to educators?
- The term and concept of *Professional Communities Learning* is introduced. Why is it different than Professional Learning Communities? What does it mean to you now? What has been added to your knowledge of professional learning? In what ways does it apply to your setting—school, district level, or county migrant regional office?

- In the context of this book and in this chapter, in what ways do you describe critical reflection, mindfulness, and *transformative learning?*
- Why is the Comprehensive Needs Assessment (CAN) in the case story such a high priority? Who needs help in moving forward to better serve migrant students and their families based on the CNA? Why and in what ways?

Going Deeper Discussion and Reflection Questions to Consider

- What are your thoughts and personal reactions about the information in this chapter? How have your reactions informed your future choices for working with migrant students in your school, the district, or migrant regional county office?
- How has the information from this chapter helped you as an educator at the local, district, or migrant regional county office? In what ways can this information be used? By you, and your school district?

GOING DEEPER

Thank you for staying with us in this journey for continuous improvement of the lives and education of our migrant students and their families. The steps in this book are designed for your use in any chapter and your school's, or migrant education program's ongoing professional learning. We include here prompts for your personal reflections as well as a provocative prompt to guide dialogic interaction between you and your colleagues.

Reflection

Take a few minutes to locate and return to your journal. Summarize your thoughts about how the concept of Professional Communities Learning (PCLs) together versus the traditional concept of Professional Learning Communities (PLCs) has informed your practice, how the *Book Study* and Palmer's Professional Development model may be used as an action plan for migrant education personnel in their efforts to continue to learn, plan, and implement effective instructional and program practices that provide access for migrant students and their families to higher levels of achievement.

- In what ways has the Book Study or Prompts for each chapter support the work of Culturally Proficient Professional Community Learning?
- What are your reactions to responding to the progression of prompts in the various chapters?

- Now that you know what you know about migrant students and their families, what are you willing to do in your role as an educator, as a migrant paraprofessional, as a migrant recruiter, or as a school district or county migrant regional personnel or director?

Dialogic Activity

Invite each member to return to their journal and in particular to their responses to the Getting Centered thinking and reflection activity. Encourage everyone to follow this protocol faithfully and in this sequence:

- What is your reaction to what you entered at that time? Yes, what are your "feelings" now about what you wrote then? (Minimally, be honest with yourself!)
- Now that you have completed the book and the attendant activities, in what ways might your response be different now?
- What have you learned about yourself as an educator through engaging with this book?
- What have you learned about your school through engaging with this book as well as with your colleagues?
- Where do you go from here?

We opened each chapter with an epigraph. We hope you enjoyed them and they contributed to your thinking. We close with a Chinese proverb:

The best time to plant a tree was 20 years ago. The second best time is now.

(Kruse, Kevin, http://www.region10.org/strategiccommunication/member-area/documents/Top100Inspirational.pdf?utm_source=HML+POST+for+May+18%2C+2015&utm_campaign=hml&utm_medium=email.)

OUR COMMITMENT TO YOU AND MIGRANT STUDENTS AND THEIR FAMILIES

In order to continue in our journey to be *Culturally Proficient,* we as authors, educators, and community members who have been involved in supporting educational and social justice issues of equity and access for migrant students and their families, as well as in the education of culturally and linguistic minority students will commit to continue to be partners with you as *Professional Community Learners.* Therefore, we invite you to tell us your success stories, the questions that you still have, the challenges as well as both your personal and professional triumphs you have had in instructing and working with migrant students. We believe that you too have committed your lives to serving migrant students and their families so they may experience access and success at the same time. We look forward to future dialogue so we may learn and teach each other to attain a social just and equitable society for all.

Reyes L. Quezada
rquezada@sandiego.edu
Fernando Rodríguez-Valls
frodriguez-valls@fullerton.edu
Randall B. Lindsey
randallblindsey@gmail.com

Appendix
Resources in Support of Migrant Education

BINATIONAL MIGRANT EDUCATION INITIATIVE (BMEI)

The goal of this program is to coordinate efforts in both sides of the border to better support migrant students and their families. Students and families face similar challenges when moving from the south part of the border to the United States and their way back to their home country. Further, a considerable number of migrant students spend half of the year in the United States and the other six months in their home countries. For more information, please check the following links: http://www2.ed.gov/admins/tchrqual/learn/binational.html; http://www.azed.gov/populations-projects/migrant-program/bi-national-transfer-document-2/

CLASSROOM, THE WE SPACE

Following a student-centered approach, two professors developed a four-week program designed to empower migrant students with critical thinking and creative skills. From the concrete to the abstract, migrant students deconstruct mathematics, language arts, and visual arts to build and create their own knowledge, which is facilitated by committed teachers and staff. For more information, please check the following link: http://epaa.asu.edu/ojs/article/view/1204/1115.

COLLEGE ASSISTANCE MIGRANT PROGRAM (CAMP)

Migrant students entering their first year at an institution of higher education (IHE) may have the support of CAMP. This program provides both financial support and a network support for migrant students use, to overcome the challenges any freshman students face in their first year at an IHE. For more information, please check the following link: http://www2.ed.gov/programs/camp/index.html.

COMPREHENSIVE NEEDS ASSESSMENT (CNA)

Under Title I, Part C, Education of Migratory Children of the Elementary and Secondary Education Act, as amended by the No Child Left Behind Act of 2001 (NCLB), State educational agencies (SEA) must deliver and evaluate Migrant Education Program (MEP)-funded services to migratory children based on a State plan that reflects the results of a current statewide comprehensive needs assessment. For more information, please check the following links: http://www2.ed.gov/admins/lead/account/comprehensive.html; http://www.cde.ca.gov/sp/me/mt/needsassessment.asp; http://www.isbe.net/bilingual/pdfs/migrant_service_plan.pdf.

GRAFFITI WALLS

The culminating project of an interdisciplinary program brings migrant students together to develop a wall reflecting their identity, their views and their inquiries. The goal is to provide a space where through dialoguing, art, and questioning, migrant students create a communal stance against the status quo and free trade. For more information, please check the following link: http://scholarscompass.vcu.edu/jstae/vol32/iss1/10/.

HIGH SCHOOL EQUIVALENCY PROGRAM (HEP)

Migrant students who are 16 years or older and are not enrolled in school receive the support of HEP's staff; thus, they can obtain a diploma, which will facilitate their entrance in post-secondary education and/or to find a job. For more information, please check the following links: http://www2.ed.gov/programs/hep/index.html; http://www.csub.edu/hep/; https://education.uoregon.edu/rou/high-school-equivalency-program.

HUMAN TRAFFICKING

The Florida Department of Education underlines the importance of reporting human trafficking. Migrant students and their families are oftentimes exposed to "involuntary servitude, peonage, debt bondage, slavery or a commercial sex act." For more information, please check the following link: http://flrecruiter.org/files/Human%20Trafficking.pdf.

LANGUAGE EXPLORERS

This curriculum is specifically designed to enhance the speaking, listening, reading, writing, critical thinking and creative skills of migrant students. In a four-week program, migrant students complete the following projects: a Bio-poem (I am); a Digital Cultural Collage; a Cultural Tag; and a Graffiti Wall. The goal is to educate migrant students to read the words and the world with critical eyes. For more information, please check the following link: http://graffitiwalls.weebly.com.

ORGANISATION FOR ECONOMIC CO-OPERATION AND DEVELOPMENT (OECD) REVIEWS ON MIGRANT EDUCATION

This document depicts the measures 30 democracies—Australia, Austria, Belgium, Canada, the Czech Republic, Denmark, Finland, France, Germany, Greece, Hungary, Iceland, Ireland, Italy, Japan, Korea, Luxembourg, Mexico, the Netherlands, New Zealand, Norway, Poland, Portugal, the Slovak Republic, Spain, Sweden, Switzerland, Turkey, the United Kingdom and the United States—created to support migrant and immigrant families. For more information, please check the following link: http://www.oecd.org/education/school/43723539.pdf.

MIGRANT EDUCATION EVEN START PROGRAM

This program exists in some states and is designed to help break the cycle of poverty and improve the literacy of participating migrant families by integrating early childhood education, adult literacy or adult basic education, and parenting education into a unified family literacy program. For more information, please check the following links: http://www2.ed.gov/programs/mees/index.html; http://ks-idr.org/migrantFamLit.html.

MIGRANT EDUCATION FAMILY BILITERACY PROGRAM (MEFBP)

This program is designed to promote and support biliteracy skills for both migrant children (ages 2–5) and their parents. Children and parents develop literacy skills in their first language—that is, Spanish, Mixteco, Zapoteco, and Hmong—and in English. The goal is to support the family's L1 as a vehicle and foundation to learn L2. For more information, please check the following link: http://www.cde.ca.gov/sp/me/mt/mefbpbackground.asp.

MIGRANT SUMMER LEADERSHIP INSTITUTES (MSLI)

Institutions of higher education work with high and middle school students in areas such as College Readiness, Science, Technology, Engineering, Art and Mathematics (STEAM). Colleges and universities host migrant students and their parents and equip them with the tools to ensure they have equal access to college and to guarantee students successfully navigate and complete their undergraduate degrees. For more information, please check the following links: http://oregonstate.edu/precollege/migrant-student-leadership-institute; http://www.csuci.edu/news/releases/2013-migrantsummerleadershipinstitute.htm.

MIGRANT STUDENTS RECORDS EXCHANGE INITIATIVE (MSIX)

MSIX is the technology that allows States to share educational and health information on migrant children who travel from State to State and who as a result, have student records in multiple States' information systems. MSIX works in concert with the existing migrant student information systems that States currently use to manage their migrant data to fulfill its mission to ensure the appropriate enrollment, placement, and accrual of credits for migrant children nationwide. For more information, please check the following link: http://www2.ed.gov/admins/lead/account/recordstransfer.html.

MIGRATION POLICY INSTITUTE (MPI)

This organization analyzes the current policies on immigration, emigration, and return migration in Canada. For more information, please check the following link: http://www.migrationpolicy.org/article/canadas-immigration-policy-focus-human-capital.

CALIFORNIA MINI-CORPS

This program trains former migrant students to tutor current migrant students. The goal is to provide individualize and differentiate instruction;

hence, migrant students are ready to meet the academic goals set by district benchmarks and state standardized tests. For more information, please check the following links: https://www.bcoe.org/divisions/california_mini-_corps; http://www.csuci.edu/academics/programs/minicorps/.

NUTRITION, HEALTH, AND SAFETY

The Migrant Education Program provides health, nutrition and safety services. For example the Migrant Education Program at Massachusetts supports migrant students and their families with eye-screening services, food services and medical assistance. For more information, please check the following link: http://www.doe.mass.edu/cnp/.

STATE SERVICE DELIVERY PLAN (SSDP)

As both an essential planning instrument and a tool for forging links to other programs and to state and local educational reform plans, the comprehensive needs assessment and service delivery plan forms the core of the new MEP. The requirements for such plans under Section 1306 clearly envision a process by which each state determines how best to fit services needed by migrant children into the state's comprehensive education reform plan developed under Goals 2000, or the plans developed by the state under other parts of the ESEA. For more information, please check the following links: http://www2.ed.gov/programs/mep/guidance/prelim_pg14.html; http://www.k12.wa.us/MigrantBilingual/Services.aspx.

SUMMER INSTITUTES

Since 2009, the Imperial Valley County Office of Education (ICOE) in partnership with San Diego State University-IV has hosted summer institutes for migrant middle school and high school students. Students attending these summer institutes work on their math, language arts, and art skills. For more information, please check the following links: http://2015icoemigrant.weebly.com.

References

Anderson, M. (2014, November/December). Diversity matters. *Leadership, 44*(2), 12–15.

Anderson, L. Gary. (2002). Reflecting on research for doctoral students in education. *Educational Researcher, 31*(7), 22–25.

Antrop-Gonzalez, R., & De Jesus, A. (2006). Toward a theory of critical care in urban small school reform: Examining structures and pedagogies of caring in two Latino community-based schools. *International Journal of Qualitative Studies in Education, 19*(4), 409–433.

Arriaga, T., & Lindsey, R. (2016). *Opening doors: An implementation template for cultural proficiency.* Thousand Oaks, CA: Corwin.

Atkins S., & Murphy K. (1994). Reflective practice. *Nursing Standard, 8*(39), 49–56.

Banks, J. A., & Park, C. (2010). Race, ethnicity, and education: The search for explanations. In P. Hill Collins & J. Solomos (Eds.), *The Sage handbook of race and ethnic studies* (pp. 383–414). London: Sage.

Bartolome, L. (2008). *Ideologies in education: Unmasking the trap of teacher neutrality.* New York, NY: Peter Lang Publishing.

Bejarano, C., & Valverde, M. (2012). From the fields to the university: Charting Educational access and success for farmworker students using a community cultural wealth framework. *Association of Mexican American Journal, 6*(2), 22–29.

Boud, D., Keogh, R., & Walker, D. (1985). *Reflection: Turning Experience into Learning.* London: Kogan Page.

Bourdieu, P. (1986). The forms of capital. In J. G. Richardson (Eds.), *Handbook of theory and research for the sociology of education* (pp. 241–258). NY: Greenwood Press.

Butte County Office of Education (2012). 2010–2011 Annual evaluation report: California Mini-Corps. Sacramento, CA.

Callahan, M. P., & Gándara, C. P. (2014). The bilingual advantage-Language, literacy and the labor US market. Multilingual Matters. Ontario, Canada.

California Department of Education (2010). California public school enrollment- district report. Retrieved April 1, 2010, from CDE Website: http://data1.cde.ca.gov/dataquest/.

California Department of Education (2013). California public school enrollment- district report. Retrieved April 1, 2015, from CDE Website: http://data1.cde.ca.gov/dataquest/.

California Department of Education (2015). State seal of biliteracy. Retrieved April 1, 2015, from CDE Website: http://www.cde.ca.gov/sp/el/er/sealofbiliteracy.asp.

Cross, T. L., Bazron, B. J., Dennis, K. W., & Isaacs, M., R. (1989). *Toward a culturally competent system of care.* Washington, DC: Georgetown University Child Development Program, Child and Adolescent Service System Program.

Cummins, J. (2000). *Language, power, and pedagogy: Bilingual children in the crossfire.* Clevedon, England: Multilingual Matters.

Cummins, J. (2013). Language and identity in multilingual schools: Constructing evidence-based instructional policies. In D. Little, C. Leung & P. Van Avermaet (Eds.) *Managing diversity in education: Languages, policies and pedagogies* (pp. 3–26). Ontario, Canada: Multilingual Matters.

Darling-Hammond, L., & McLaughlin, M. (1995, April). Policies that support professional development in an era of reform. *Phi Delta Kappan, 76,* 597–603.

Dantas, L. M., & Manyak, C. P. (2010). Home-school connections in a multicultural society: Learning from and with culturally and linguistically diverse families. New York, NY: Routledge.

Delgado Bernal, D. (2001). Learning and living pedagogies of the home: The Mestizo consciousness of Chicana students. *International Journal of Qualitative Studies in Education, 14*(5), 623–639.

Delgado Bernal, D. (2002). Critical race theory, LatCrit theory and critical racedgendered epistemologies: Recognizing students of color as holders and creators of knowledge. *Qualitative Inquiry, 8*(1), 105–126.

Delpit, L. (2005). *Other's People Children: Cultural Conflict in the classroom.* New York, NY: The New Press.

Dewey, J. (1933). How we think. Buffalo, New York. Collier Books, McMillian. Education in Changing Contexts/Ross Institute Summer Academy 2009. https://www.youtube.com/watch?v=SzhJrohxHiA.

Epstein, J. L. (2011). *School, family, and community partnerships: Preparing educators and improving schools* (2nd edition). Boulder, CO: Westview.

Epstein, J. L., et al. (2009). *School, family, and community partnerships: Your handbook for action* (3rd edition). Thousand Oaks, CA: Corwin.

Epstein, J. L., & Salinas, K. (2004). Schools as learning communities. *Educational Leadership, 61*(8), 12–18.

Freire, P. (1981). *Education for critical consciousness.* NY: Continuum.

Freire, P. (1986). *Pedagogy of the oppressed.* NY: Continuum.

Gándara, C., P. (2010, February). "The Latino education crisis." *Meeting students where they are, 67*(5), 24–30. *Educational Leadership.*

Gay, G. (2000). *Culturally responsive teaching: Theory, research, and practice.* New York, NY: Teachers College Press.

Gibson, M. A., & Bejinez, L. F. (2002). Dropout prevention: How migrant education supports Mexican youth. *The Journal of Latinos in Education, 1*(3), 155–175.

Gibson, M. A., & Hidalgo, N. (2009). Bridges to success in high school for migrant youth. *Teachers College Record, 111*(3), 683–711.

Giroux, H. A. (1985). Teachers as transformative intellectuals. *Social Education, 2,* 376–379.

Goodwin, L. A. (2012). Globalization and the preparation of quality teachers: Rethinking knowledge domains for teaching. In Quezada, R. L. (Eds.), *Internationalization of teacher education: Creating globally competent teachers and teacher educators for the 21st century* (pp. 19–33). London, UK: Routledge.

Gonzalez, N. (2005). The hybridity of funds of knowledge. In N. Gonzalez, L. C. Moll & C. Amanti (Eds.), *Funds of knowledge: Theorizing practices in households, communities and classrooms* (pp. 29–46). NJ: Lawrence Erlbaum.

Gonzalez, N., Moll, L., & Amanti, C. (2005). Introduction: Theorizing practices. In N. Gonzalez, L. C. Moll & C. Amanti. (Eds.), *Funds of Knowledge: Theorizing practices in households, communities and classrooms* (pp. 1–28). NJ: Lawrence Erlbaum.

Green, E. P. (2003). The undocumented: Educating the children of migrant workers in America. *Bilingual Research Journal, 27*(1), 51–71.

Heifetz, R. A. (2010, Spring). Adaptive work. *The Journal Kansas Leadership Center,* 72–77.

Henderson, A. T., & Mapp, K. L. (2002). A new wave of evidence: The impact of school, family and community connections on student achievement (Research Synthesis).

Herrera, G. S., & Murray, G. K. (2005). *Mastering ESL and bilingual methods: Differentiated instruction for culturally and linguistically diverse (CLD) students.* Boston, MA: Pearson.

Hess, B. (2007). Children in the fields an American problem. Association of Farmworker Programs. Washington, DC.

Hinkle, G. E., Tipton, R. L., & Tutchings. (1979). *Who cares? Who counts? A national study of migrant student needs.* Austin, Texas: St. Edwards University.

Hogg, L. (2011). Funds of knowledge: An investigation of coherence within the literature. *Teaching and Teacher Education, 27*(3), 666–677.

Holmes, M. S. (2013). *Fresh fruits, broken bodies-Migrant workers in the United States.* Berkeley, CA: University of California Press.

Hooks, B. (2008). *Belonging: A culture of place.* New York, NY: Routledge.

Hord, M. S., & Sommers, W. (2008). *Leading professional learning communities: Voices from research and practice.* Thousand Oaks, CA: Corwin.

Hord, M. S. (2009). Professional learning communities-Educators work together toward a shared purpose-Improved student learning. *National Staff Development Council, 30*(1), 40–43.

Intercultural Development Research Institute. Education equity and reform goals. Retrieved November 3, 2015, from www.http://idra.org.

Jeynes, W. (2012). A meta-analysis of the efficacy of different types of parental involvement programs for urban students. *Urban Education, 47,* 706–742.

Kiely, R. (2005). A transformative learning model for service-learning: A longitudinal case study. *Michigan Journal of Community Service Learning, 12,* 5–22.

Kozoll, R. H., Osborne, M. D., & García, G. E. (2003). Migrant worker children: conceptions of homelessness and implications for education. *Qualitative Studies in Education, 16*(4), 567–585.

Kruse, K., Retrieved January 10 from: http://www.region10.org/strategiccommunication/memberarea/documents/Top100Inspirational.pdf?utm_source=HML+POST+for+May+18%2C+2015&utm_campaign=hml&utm_medium=email.

Ladson-Billings, G. (2001). *Crossing over to Canaan: The journey of new teachers in diverse classrooms*. San Francisco: Jossey Bass.

Ladson-Billings, G. (1995). But that's just good teaching! The case for culturally relevant pedagogy. *Theory into Practice, 31*, 160–166.

Langer, J. E. (1997). *The power of mindful learning*. Reading, MA: Addison-Wesley.

Lave, J., & Wenger, E. (1991). *Situated learning: Legitimate peripheral participation*. New York, NY: Cambridge University Press.

Learning Forward (2011). *Standards for professional learning*. Oxford, Ohio: Author. Retrieved from http://learningforward.org/standards-for-professional-learning.

Lévinas, E. (2005). *Humanism of the Other*. Chicago, IL: University of Illinois Press.

Lindsey, B., D & Lindsey, B. R. (2014, November/December). Cultural proficiency: Why ask why? *Leadership, 44*(2), 24–27 & 37.

Lindsey, B. D., Jungwirth, L. D., Pahl, V. N. C., & Lindsey, R. B. (2009). *Culturally proficient learning communities: Confronting inequities through collaborative curiosity*. Thousand Oaks, CA: Corwin.

Lindsey, B. R., Nuri R. K., & Terrell, D., R. (2009). *Cultural Proficiency: A Manual for School Leaders*, 3rd edition. Thousand Oaks, CA: Corwin.

Lindsey, B. D., Lindsey, B. R., Hord, M. S., & Von Frank, V. (2015). *Reach the highest standard in professional learning – outcomes*, Thousand Oaks, CA: Corwin and Learning Forward.

Lindsey, B. D., Kearney, M. K., Estrada, D., Terrell, D. R., & Lindsey, B. R. (2015). *A cultural proficient response to the common core: Ensuring equity through professional learning*. Corwin. Thousand Oaks, CA.

Linsky, M., & Heifetz, R. A. (2002). *Leadership on the line: Staying alive through the dangers of leading*. Boston, MA: Harvard Business Review Press.

Lundy-Ponce, G. (2010). Migrant Students: What we need to know to help them. Author. Retrieved from http://www.ldonline.org/article/36286?theme=print.

Mathur, S. (2011). Educating the migrant Child: Professional development for teachers of young children of seasonal farm workers *The Journal of Multiculturalism in Education, 7*(3), 1–16.

Mezirow, J. (1991). *Transformative Dimensions of Adult Learning*. San Francisco, CA: Jossey-Bass.

Mezirow, J. (1997). Transformative learning: Theory to practice. *New directions for Adult and Continuing Education, 74*, 5–12.

Moll, L. C. (1992). Bilingual classroom studies and community analysis: Some recent trends. *Educational Researcher, 21*(2), 20–24.

National Education Association of the United States-Office of Minority Community Outreach. (2010). A national imperative for head start students and their families. NEA, Washington, D.C.

Nieto, S. (2006). *Teaching as political work: Learning from courageous and caring teachers*. Child Development Institute. Sarah Lawrence College. The Longfellow Lecture Occasional Papers.

Nieto, S. (2008). *Affirming Diversity: The Sociopolitical Context of Multicultural Education*, New York: Allyn & Bacon Publishers

Nieto, S. (2010). *The light in their eyes: Creating multicultural learning communities* (10th edition.) New York: Teachers College Press.

Nieto, S. (2013). *Finding joy in teaching students of diverse backgrounds: Culturally responsive and socially just practices in U.S. classrooms.* Heinemann, Portsmouth, NH.

Nieto, S. (2015 October). Teaching students of diverse backgrounds: Culturally responsive and socially just practices in U.S. classrooms. Lecture at the University of San Diego. San Diego, CA.

O'Sullivan, E. (2003). Bringing a perspective of transformative learning to a global consumption. *International Journal of Consumer Studies, 27*(4), 326–330.

Palmer, P. J. (2007). *The courage to teach: Exploring the inner landscape of a teacher's life (10th Anniversary Edition).* San Francisco, CA: Jossey-Bass.

Patel, L. (2012). *Youth held at the border: Immigration, education, and the politics of inclusion.* New York, NY: Teachers College Press.

Patterson, K., Grenny, J., McMillan, R., & Switzler, A. (2011). *Crucial conversations: Tools for talking when skates are high.* New York, NY: McGraw-Hill Education.

Penetito, W. (2001). If only we knew … contextualizing Māori knowledge. In B. Webber & L. Mitchell (Eds.). *Early childhood education for a democratic society: Conference proceedings* (pp. 17–25). Wellington, New Zealand: Council for Educational Research.

Ponlop, D. (2010). *Rebel Buddha: A guide to a revolution of mind.* Boston, MA. Shambhala Publications. Inc.

Quezada, R. (1991). Preparation of instructional skills for migrant Mini-Corps teacher assistants: Comparing perceptions among master teachers and college coordinators. Unpublished Dissertation. Northern Arizona University.

Quezada, R., Lindsey, B. R., & Lindsey, B. D. (2012). Culturally proficient practice-Supporting educators of English learning students. Thousand Oaks, CA: Corwin Press.

Quezada, R. (2014 Spring/Summer–August). Family-school, & community engagement and partnerships: Working with culturally diverse families. *Multicultural Education, 21*(3 & 4), 2–4.

Quezada, R., Alexandrowicz, V., & Molina, S. (2015). Family, school, community engagement and partnerships: An imperative for k-12, and colleges of education in the development of 21st century educators. UK. Routledge.

Rodríguez-Valls, F., Montoya, M., & Valenzuela, P. (2014). Biliteracy summer schools: Breaking the cycle of monolingualism in migrant families. *Childhood Education, 90*(2), 107–115.

Rodríguez-Valls, F. (2009). Culturally relevant poetry: Creating *Esperanza* (hope) with stanzas. *Multicultural Education, 17*(1), 10–13.

Rodríguez-Valls, F., Kofford, S., & Morales, E. (2012). Graffiti walls: Migrant students and the art of communicative languages. *Journal of Social Theory in Art Education, 32*, 96–111.

Rodríguez-Valls, F., & Ponce, G. (2013). Classroom, the we space: Developing student-centered practices for second language learners (SLL). *Education Policy Analysis Archives*, *21*(55). http://epaa.asu.edu/ojs/article/view/1204/1115.

Rodríguez-Valls, F., & Torres, C. (2014). Partnerships and networks in migrant education: Empowering migrant families to support their children's success. *Multicultural Education*, *21*(3 & 4), 34–38.

Shealey, M.W., Alvarez McHatton, P., & Wilson, V. (2011). Moving beyond disproportionality: the role of culturally responsive teaching in special education. *Teaching Education*, *22*(4), 377–396, DOI: 10.1080/10476210.2011.591376.

Sinek, S. (2009). *Start With Why*. New York: The Penguin Group.

Suárez-Orozco, C., Suárez-Orozco, M., & Todorova, I. (2010). *Learning a new land: Immigrant students in American society*. Cambridge, MA: Belknap Press.

Spaulding, S., Carolino, B., & Amen, K. A. (2004). *Immigrant students and secondary school reform: Compendium of best practices*. Washington, D.C.: Council of Chief State School Officers (State Services and Technical Assistance Division).

Terrell, R. D., & Lindsey, R. B. (2009). *Culturally proficient leadership: The personal journey begins within*. Thousand Oaks, CA: Corwin Press.

Terrell, R. D., & Lindsey, R. B. (2015). *Culturally proficient leadership: Doing what's right for students – all students*. In Portelli, John P., & Griffiths, Darrin, Eds. (2014). Key Questions for Educational Leaders. Burlington, ON: Word & Deeds Publ. Inc.

Theoharris, G. (2007). Social justice educational leaders and resistance: Toward a theory of social justice leadership. *Educational Administration Quarterly*, *43*(2), 221–258.

U.S. Department of Education, National Center for Education Statistics. (2010). *The Condition of Education*. 2010 (NCES 2010-028), Indicator 5.

U. S. Department of Education (2011). Office of the Under Secretary, Planning and Evaluation Service, Elementary and Secondary Education Division, *The Same High Standards for Migrant Students: Holding Title I Schools Accountable*, Executive Summary, Washington, D.C., 2002.

U.S. Department of Education (2006). Migrant Education Program Annual Report: Eligibility, Participation, Services and Achievement.

U. S. Department of Education (2015). Every Student Succeeds Act. Retrieved December 15 from http://www.ed.gov/essa.

Van Baalen, P. J., & Moratis, L. T. (2012). *Management education in the network economy: Its context, content and organization*. Boston, MA: Springer.

Veaco, L. (1973). *The effect of paraprofessional assistance on the academic achievement of migrant children*. Unpublished dissertation. University of the Pacific.

Vocke, S. K., & Pfeiffer, S. A. (2009). Building community for migrant education services through family literacy and farm worker outreach. *The Tapestry Journal*, *1*(1), 30–39.

ŽiŽek, S. (2014). *Demanding the impossible*. Malden, MA: Polity Press.

Index

About the Authors

Dr. Reyes L. Quezada is professor at the University of San Diego, in the Department of Learning and Teaching in the School of Leadership and Education Sciences. His teaching and research focus are in bilingual education, equity, cultural proficiency, parent involvement, international education, inclusion, and diversity. His publications include journals and chapter contributions on international teacher education, bilingual/multicultural education, peace education, character education, home-school community involvement, teacher certification, and adventure-based education and counseling.

He has extensive experience in state, national, and international boards, such as the International Council for the Education of Teachers (ICET); as past president of the California Council for Teacher Education; as vice president for the American Association of Colleges for Teacher Education (AACTE); as the California representative for the Association of Teacher Educators (ATE). He is a governing board member for several journals and the associate editor for *Teacher Education Quarterly*. He has been a California Commission on Teacher Credentialing-Committee on Accreditation (COA) member for the past eight years, and on the San Bernardino Equal Opportunity Commission.

Dr. Fernando Rodríguez-Valls is associate professor at California State University, Fullerton. He has created partnerships with school districts, local educational agencies, and universities to develop and implement community-based [bi]literacy programs. Rodríguez-Valls's work focuses on equitable instructional practices for second language learners and migrant students as well as on the sociocultural factors affecting their academic achievement, educational continuity, and school engagement.

Dr. Randall B. Lindsey is emeritus professor at California State University, Los Angeles. He has a practice centered on educational consulting and issues related to diversity. He has served as a teacher, an administrator, and an executive director of a nonprofit corporation. He served for 17 years at California State University, Los Angeles, in the Division of Administration and Counseling. He served as chair of the Division of Administration and Counseling and as director of the Regional Assistance Centers for Educational Equity, a regional race desegregation assistance center. He has coauthored several books and articles on cultural proficiency.

35351637R00114